D1503019

THE BEVERLY HILLS MEDICAL DIET & LONG-LIFE ANTI-STRESS PROGRAM

Arnold Fox, M.D.

Foreword by

Robert S. Mendelsohn, M.D.
author of
Confessions of a Medical Heretic

Chain - Pinkham Books

I

Chain-Pinkham Books
6414 Cambridge Street
St. Louis Park, Minnesota 55426

CONTENTS

DEDICATION

To:

Minnie May and Benjamin (the past).

Hannah (the present).

Howard and Robin, Eric, Barry, Steve, Pamela, Barbara, and Hiam (the future).

With Special Acknowledgements:

Jeanne Schwartz, Shirley Albert and
Hannah Fox for always striving for the very best for the patients.
And Cindy Turpin Owen, Stan Ginsburg for taking good care of
the manuscript.

FOREWORD

BY

Robert S. Mendelsohn, M.D.

Solid good sense is a rare bird when doctors talk about diets. The fact is that here, as in other parts of the medical field, our brotherhood seems to be guided by a conspiracy to hush up the obvious. In diets, the obvious is nutrition; yet very few of the physicians who write diet books appear inclined to intelligently address themselves to that vital, all-important question.

The reason is simple. Doctors are too uneducated in the subject to appreciate the value of nutrition. Consequently, they either ignore it altogether or they lead crusades for diets that are either ineffective or dangerous, or both.

It is not surprising, therefore, that the most popular doctor-prescribed diets in recent years have been failures. Year after year we see such books flood the market. But with Dr. Fox's landmark work, the end of the inundation may be in sight.

Nutrition is inseparable from health and even more tragic than the failure to maintain weight loss are the hazards to which the followers of the popular high-protein diets have been exposed. Here Dr. Fox is truly illuminating.

The dangers of ketosis, as he has well elaborated, may be of far greater consequence than even the disappointment in failing to maintain weight loss. The burden the recent popular diets place on the heart, and the other long-term health risks they pose are only now coming into the public forum. In addition, Dr. Fox has brought into clear focus the relationship between nutrition and stress.

As a physician I agree with the Beverly Hills Medical Diet because the only successful weight-loss program is one that is in tune with man's nutritional needs and his physical and mental wellbeing.

Dr. Arnold Fox has given us a scientifically valid, highly literate, historically-compatible, rationally-based, easy-to-follow prescription for safe, effective, practical, satisfying — and permanent — weight loss and good health.

THE BEVERLY HILLS MEDICAL DIET

IF YOU'RE IN DOUBT...

about your general health or minor but persistent problems; if you are on prescription drugs or suffer from serious ailments – in other words if your physical condition is not altogether satisfactory – you are advised to seek medical consultation in following the Beverly Hills Medical Diet.

Tell your doctor what the Beverly Hills Medical Diet is all about and request him to adapt your medical requirements to the diet.

CHAPTER ONE:

BHMD: THE BETTER WAY

I HAVE SEEN THE PROOF

With the Beverly Hills Medical Diet you will lose weight. As much as ten pounds, or more, in two weeks.

With my Long-Life Anti-Stress Program you will feel better. Better than you ever thought possible.

With my program of sound nutrition you will live longer. And you will *stay* slim.

Too good to be true?

Hardly.

I have seen the proof.

I have seen people shed ten, twenty, thirty or more pounds. I have seen them with their new looks take on a new glow. I have seen them suddenly face a world that looked better to them – because *they* looked better. I still have my office in Beverly Hills. But because of the success of the Beverly Hills Medical Diet I no longer practice medicine in the usual fashion.

I have found a better way.

There is the BHMD "Plunge," in which you lose ten or more pounds in fourteen days.

There is the BHMD "Everyday" weight loss, in which you drop a comfortable three pounds a week.

Then there is the "Maintenance" program, a nutritional approach to keeping your desired weight and achieving stress-free longevity.

But I don't tell people to diet.

I tell them to eat for the rest of their lives.

THEY WERE AMAZED

I call my weight-loss program the Beverly Hills Medical Diet. I took that name because it was in that glamorous but stressful town that my practice showed me the necessity for a healthly, balanced and permanent method of weight reduction.

The people who came to my office were those that many would tend to envy. They were wealthy, successful and lived lives filled with activity. Yet, many had the same problems faced by the other eighty million overweight Americans.

I am a doctor with a scientist's education, trained to observe and verify. And if I speak of the Beverly Hills Medical Diet with a little excitement it is only because of my extreme delight in its success.

I have seen the diet work!

I have seen people who followed it become slim and stay slim. I have been pleased to see them look better and more self-assured. They have become nothing less than enthusiasts who swear by the BHMD.

The BHMD is now a part of their lives. They have experienced fast weight loss and better health. They are following the BHMD and never gain an ounce. That's because the BHMD is not just a diet. It is a healthier way of eating and a better way of living.

THERE WAS SOMETHING I COULD DO

The success of my program has been as welcome to me as it has been to my patients. For the past twenty years I have practiced internal medicine. I am associated with two cardiologists. There are many satisfactions that make my profession worthwhile. But for much of my practice I was frustrated. I saw too many people ruin themselves by their eating habits.

They were wrecking their health with food. The wrong foods and too much of them.

I wondered if there was something I could do. I realized that with all my medical training and practice I also needed to become a nutritionist. I discovered that the subject of stress required intense study and investigation.

It is no secret that while we have eliminated the historic illnesses, we are struck down by the "modern" plagues – cancer, heart disease, strokes, diabetes and arthritis. These diseases don't just happen. The evidence overwhelmingly shows that most of today's illnesses are due to poor nutrition, poor health habits and a poor handling of stress.

Over the years I realized that if I were to help my patients live healthier and longer they would require a program combining proper nutritional approaches with a regimen reducing stress. They needed to become not only physiologically but also psychologically fit. Thus was born the Beverly Hills Medical Diet and Long-Life Anti-Stress Plan.

BHMD=BHMD (Beverly Hills Medical Diet=Better Health Medical Diet

You will lose weight fast and easy. You will be able to take your choice of many permissible and delicious foods. You will feel in the pink of psychological wellbeing. You will stay slim and trim. And you will live young to an old age.

How?

Because the Beverly Hills Medical Diet modifies your way of eating. You adopt a diet that works. On the BHMD you develop a whole new pattern of food consumption.

Your plate will no longer groan under heaps of rich viands. Nor will your body groan in turn. Your diet will be more closely akin to that of the hardy and sturdy peoples who, though poor, have flourished and lived to a ripe old age in the less favored regions of the world.

GET OFF THE ROLLER COASTER

Unlike the run-of-the-mill or faddist diets, the BHMD does not totally limit carbohydrates. I *do not* ban the dishes which the faddists and mistaken nutritionists rule taboo. I believe that these types of popular diet are to blame for that most excrutiating of dietary woes: the "roller coaster" effect of weight loss.

I once had a patient who had three suits – for *regular* weight, *overweight,* and *greatly overweight.* He used all of the suits throughout the year. It seemed funny when I heard him tell this story, but it wasn't at all funny when I sat with him last year in the hospital before and after his coronary by-pass surgery. It is well known that during the weight gain *after* weight loss considerably extra fat and cholesterol is laid down in the coronary arteries.

We know what a roller coaster does. It goes up and down and in circles, and afterwards you feel dizzy and confused. Ninety out of 100 dieters gain their full weight back again within five years.

The faddist and regular diets operate like the "roller coaster." They take your weight down and up, up and down, and once your feet hit the scales again you are likely to feel rattled and discouraged.

But what is far more serious, the ride may impair your health. The "up-and-down" method practiced by many people actually results in depositing *more* fat on the body and in the arteries. That's what happened to my patient with the three-size wardrobe.

On the BHMD your weight doesn't bounce up and down like a yo-yo. There is none of that "slim-or-sink." You stay afloat at the proper body trim for as long as you live.

ROUND ONE: C.C. vs. "KILLER" PROTEIN

I have chosen a metaphor from the boxing ring to underscore the key to the BHMD. There is no doubt in my mind which of the two diet contenders my money is on. What Muhammed Ali said about himself I say about C.C.: "It is the greatest."

My diet calls for a nutritional approach high in *Complex Carbohydrates.* At the same time it seeks to score a "knock-out" over the Protein.

When C.C. wins, your health is in the chips.

When C.C. gains the title your body looks and feels like a million dollars.

TIME BOMB

I consider the emphasis on high-protein diets like telling someone to bury a time bomb in his body. The steaks and chops, the butter and cheese are the

4

elements in that time bomb. By consuming these products you are planting an explosive around the cardiovascular system and the heart.

There is a fuse, too. That fuse is your protein habit.

In making this statement I realize that I have already antagonized 95% of the diet doctors and nutritionists who swear by the High-Protein Bible. But I am not displeased about their anger. I have seen too much evidence of the damage caused by their advocacy to take their sputtering seriously.

Thus I have no sympathy for those doctors who blithely prescribe a high-protein diet to their desperate patients. Frankly, I feel ashamed for what they do to medical standards.

I have seen gentlemen with M.D. behind their names and with the most sincere smile hook their patients on the protein habit. I have asked myself whether they had forgotten their school books. Whether they had an inkling of the tremendous load they were putting on the patient's digestive and metabolic system. Whether they knew that the high-protein intake is one of the reasons for the dismal health statistics in our country!

In the following chapters you will learn some astonishing facts concerning the hazards of the high-protein habit. For now, let's look quickly at. . .

KETOSIS!

As with high-protein foods, the BHMD turns its nose down on cholesterol. It rejects fats. It positively spurns refined carbohydrates, like white flour or sugar.

On the BHMD you stick to the foods that provide the best sources of energy. Edibles that are close to natural food products. Menu items containing starch and fibers. Dishes rich in minerals and natural vitamins. The BHMD offers an extensive variety of tasty, low-calorie foods that can be permanently adopted in your total diet plan.

By now you know that I am talking about foods high in *Complex Carbohydrates.*

Perhaps my fervor for C.C. sounds exaggerated. "It may be so, but does he have to shout it from the roof top," I can almost hear the reader say.

My response to this is, "Yes, I wish I could shout it from the roof of every American house. With their large amounts of protein, fats, cholesterol and refined carbohydrates Americans are killing themselves."

A diet high in Complex Carbohydrates takes off weight and may even result in a natural burning off of *more* calories. A new study on rats reported

5

in the prestigious *Science* magazine this year showed conclusively that weight is lost much more effectively through a diet low in fat and protein and rich in Complex Carbohydrates, such as grains, vegetables and fruits. Of two sets of animals, one group eating 25 percent higher in protein than the other group, was found after eight weeks to weigh 22 percent more than the rats fed on a low-protein diet.

Rapid weight loss is the chief ingredient in the BHMD. But just as important are the additional values the diet offers. The C.C. diet will give you a new figure, but what's more, it will prolong and enrich your life by reducing stress.

If we take the average American executive we see a man exhibiting two prominent characteristics. He is overweight and his body suffers from stress. This stress is aggravated seriously by a dangerous side-effect produced by his high-protein diet. It is called *Ketosis*.

The reduction of ketosis is one of the chief benefits of the diet high in Complex Carbohydrates. My Long-Life Anti-Stress Plan is part of the BHMD. Therefore, we shall hear more about that stress-producing condition, *Ketosis*.

LIKE TAKING PILLS WITHOUT A PRESCRIPTION

That's my term for the unwholesome regimen which the well-known proponents of protein have spread among diet-conscious Americans. Typical of these are the Scarsdale and Dr. Atkins diets.

The shortcuts they promise take the dieter on a roundabout, disappointing and dangerous road. The high-protein diet they advocate disrupts homeostasis, the body's balance, resulting in stress, tension, nausea, and sleeplessness.

Having studied their works I believe the government should set up a new F.D.A. – A Federal Diet Administration. This agency would test the effects of the diets, and especially determine whether they reduce the chances of heart, liver and gall bladder disease, cancer and hypertension.

What irks me most about the anti-carbohydrate diets is the pit of disappointment they dig for the unsuspecting user. The dieter embarks on these programs desperate to lose fat. He happily notes his initial loss of weight.

Unfortunately his joy is a delusion.

He does not realize that what he has dropped is mostly water. And because he is losing water, the weight loss is temporary, so that he is really riding that roller coaster we mentioned earlier.

In my diet I say *drop fat, not water.*

If my Federal Diet Administration ever comes about its first order of business would be to look into the dangers posed by the weight loss resulting from the protein programs. It is for a very good reason that the Scarsdale regimen warns the user not to stay on it for more than two weeks. The dieter on this regimen, nutritionally speaking, is liable to overload his heart with stress. That's why I decided that no diet plan could be complete without dealing with the stress factor.

WOULDN'T IT BE NICE. . .

To moderate your eating habits while feeling good? To get off the roller coaster and on the straight road to dietary wellbeing? To eat and know that you are slimming? To stay slim and rejoice in feeling good and relaxed?

With the BHMD and Long-Life Anti-Stress Plan I have achieved what the protein diets promise but don't deliver. In the BHMD, for instance, there are no artificial sweeteners, as there are in Scarsdale and Atkins. The BHMD is a natural diet in harmony with nature and the human body. It helps you turn those bulging lines into the neat contours you crave. And because of your remodeled eating patterns the weight loss is permanent.

ONE MORE WORD TO THE WISE

Before we get into the *C.C.* of the book, I should point out there are no miracles in nature. Nature works marvelously according to a plan that commands our reverence. But it has no miracles, as science will tell you. Likewise, the BHMD, which takes nature as its model, does not provide anything exceeding the bounds of the possible.

As the director of the American Institute of Health in Beverly Hills I run a series of mini-clinics in which people learn how to stay healthy and vigorous. There they are told straight away that I do not offer a chocolate-flavored miracle program. Instead I propose, as I do in my regular practice, that they and I become partners in health.

7

You are the key to the New Health, which you can obtain by following the Anti-Stress Beverly Hills Medical Diet.

Before you embark on your journey to the new, healthier and longer-living you, test your nutritional practices with a self-nutritional survey.

SELF-NUTRITIONAL SURVEY

Too many check (✓) marks indicate your nutritional practices need revising.

Check only the questions that you would answer as yes.

Check

( ) 1. I know what good nutrition is but it is difficult for me to apply this knowledge in a consistent manner.

( ) 2. I must learn more about nutrition so I can eat better.

( ) 3. I have specific problems.

( ) 4. My nutrition is not good.

( ) 5. I have been put on a restricted diet before.

( ) 6. I have a history of indigestion.

( ) 7. I have a history of constipation.

( ) 8. I have a history of diarrhea.

( ) 9. I have a history of excess gas.

( ) 10. I am overweight.

( ) 11. I am seriously overweight.

( ) 12. I have had trouble losing weight.

( ) 13. I gain weight easily.

( ) 14. I frequently feel listless after eating.

( ) 15. I often have cravings for food I shouldn't eat.

( ) 16. I put salt on my foods.

( ) 17. I crave sugar and sugary foods.

( ) 18. I often eat high fat, high cholesterol foods.

( ) 19. I eat, chew and swallow rapidly.

( ) 20. I don't, as a rule, eat breakfast.

( ) 21. I often eat while working or "on the run."

( ) 22. I feel better immediately after eating, only to slump later.

( ) 23. I like to eat late at night. It helps calm me.

( ) 24. If I go without eating too long I get tense or irritable.

( ) 25. I don't usually read food labels.

( ) 26. Let's face it – I'm a junk food junkie.

( ) 27. I need that coffee in the morning to get going.

( ) 28. I eat pretty well except I don't know when to stop.

( ) 29. I eat lots of canned or convenience foods.

( ) 30. I have food allergies.

CHAPTER TWO:

INSIDE THE BHMD: THE SECRET OF RAPID WEIGHT LOSS

WHAT'S WRONG WITH US?

There's something wrong with us. When 80 million Americans are overweight – that is, nearly one in two – then I think I have reason to state that there is definitely something terribly wrong in our diet and the way we eat.

Despite several decades of diet consciousness the chubby statistics prevail to this day. Since the Second World War, Americans have been on and off an inconceivable variety of regimen.

They've been on diets exclusively devoted to bananas and milk. They've been on others which advocated little more than sucking on a grapefruit. They've ingested the growth hormone from the urine of pregnant women. They've even tried to cut poundage by stapling their ears, in the hope that by wiggling the stapled lobe hunger would disappear.

Dietwise, you name it and Americans have given it a whirl. They've adopted the gospel that calories don't count and they've ballyhooed others that say calories do. They've been on a drinking man's diet. They've followed the Air Force Diet. They've eaten high-cholesterol and low-cholesterol, saturated and unsaturated fats, liquid and solid, fiber and non-fiber. In short, they've tried everything and they're still fighting the same bulges.

The sad story is that Americans pile their fat back on as soon as each diet has

9

run its faddish course.

But let's travel to certain regions of Africa and Asia, or some parts of Eastern Europe. There we see an altogether different picture.

The people there may not have our comforts. They may not have our variety of foods. But on the other hand we do not see them felled by heart attacks or strokes. Our most common types of cancer are hardly known among them. They rarely suffer hemmorhoids. They are unfamiliar with certain colon diseases or phlebitis. What's more, they're not obese.

Now let's see what happens when these same people forsake their native nutrition and come to the United States. In the most advanced country in the world they suddenly get sick. If they do not directly succumb to the diseases from which Americans suffer, they do not on the whole feel as well as formerly.

What happened?

Nothing, except that they've adopted our way of living and eating. As a result, they've become prone to stress, with its incidence of heart attacks. And they've become susceptible to obesity, with its incidence of "diet books" that don't work.

All these facts I learned because I used to sign three death certificates a week. This dismal routine set me in pursuit of the relation between nutrition, obesity and stress. It put me on the trail where each mortality was a clue. It set me tracking down the element in the daily sustenance of people who were not fat. I wanted to know more about these hardy specimens that were happily spared the degenerative illnesses from which Americans die.

What I came up with was that the thinner and healthier Africans and Asians were eating diets rich in unrefined carbohydrates. While I was counseling obese patients, they were staying slim on corn meal, bananas, beans, potatoes, rich starch and high-fiber vegetables. They were enjoying longevity, while I was signing death certificates for people who had been punishing their bodies with beef, lamb, fish, eggs and sugar.

THE MYTH OF "STARCH"

With the BHMD I hope to dispel a myth Americans have been laboring under too long. It is the mistaken belief that "starchy" foods cause obesity. Somehow the idea has gotten around that starch is incompatible with weight loss and sound eating principles.

Here I shall sum up the credo of the BHMD in a nut shell: "Starchy" foods, as long as they are unrefined, are chockful of Complex Carbohydrates. Therefore, the BHMD sets before you a hearty feast of those Complex Carbohydrates and

10

fiber-laden foods for, 1) rapid and permanent weight reduction, 2) for longevity, 3) for stress removal, and 4) for general health.

The BHMD shows you how by way of the Complex Carbohydrates a few simple changes in diet enable you to lose weight fast while reducing the risk of cardiovascular disease. You learn to recognize the risk factors and how to avoid them. You learn how to read labels, how to alter favorite recipes, and how to eat away from home.

The BHMD will slim you and make you health-conscious without upsetting your life-style.

THE ENEMIES OF BHMD

Since the issue is so clouded with misinformation, and especially since carbohydrates have been made the villain in so many popular diets, let us examine the myth and its hazards. Six years ago the U.S. Department of Agriculture interviewed some 2,500 homemakers and found that only three per cent had a general nutritional knowledge. On the BHMD it is as important to know what you eat as why you eat what you eat.

We have already seen that a low-carbohydrate diet is often another word for a high-protein, high-fat and high-cholesterol intake. Just how this type of diet is able to promote a temporary weight loss is shown best in the theory behind the most popular of the contemporary slimming manuals. These are *Dr. Atkins' Diet Revolution* and *The Complete Scarsdale Medical Diet.*

First off, I should say that there is very little "revolutionary" about a diet that an English surgeon, William Harvey, prescribed for his patients more than a century ago.

Secondly, I hope to dismiss, once and for all, the chief contention of the "revolutionary" diets.

Thirdly, I shall explain the *Three S's* of the BHMD. Why it's *Simple, Safe,* and *Speedy.*

"SLEIGHT-OF-FAT"

The high-protein/low-carbohydrate diets advocated by Atkins and Scarsdale have perfected a technique for which I have coined a phrase. They use what I call a "sleight-of-fat."

The English Dr. Harvey got the low-carbohydrate ball rolling by cutting out

11

sweet and starchy foods, restricting his Victorian clientele to a high-protein and fat intake. But it was up to his modern successors, like the Atkins and Scarsdale diets, to claim that the high-protein/low-carbohydrate fare breaks down the body's fat stores faster than normal.

When that happens, according to our high priests of protein, fragments of carbon are released. In the Atkins diet these fragments are called FMH, Fat Mobilizing Hormone. We shall stick to the scientific name, "ketone bodies," which are basically nothing more than poorly burned fatty acids. The resulting condition – the metabolized or partially burned fat fragments – is the "ketosis" we touched upon earlier.

According to the Scarsdale, Dr. Atkins and similar diets, ketone production means that excess fat is being pulled out of your fat reserves. The ketones, according to Scarsdale, transform your body into a "fat-burning machine." But it would be far more accurate to say that the ketones turn the body into a sprinkling system.

The ketones stimulate urinary losses, and this is what I meant by my somewhat facetious "sleight-of-fat." The "miracle" of fast weight reduction promised by the low-carbohydrate/high-protein diets is nothing more than a change in water balance. Moreover, the water-loss occurs primarily in the diet's initial 8-10 day period. After that the "sprinkling system" sputters to a halt, while the fat largely remains where it has always been.

YOUR BODY IS A TEMPLE

The Beverly Hills Medical Diet runs counter to the "revolutionists." It begins where the high-protein promises leave off. It scorns to use a "faucet" technique in which the well soon runs dry. With its emphasis on Complex Carbohydrates, the BHMD attacks obesity at its soft spot, if you will. That soft spot is not liquid but fat.

There is just no getting around it. Fat is the most compact package of calories the body stores. These "packages" are contained in the outsized bulges you wish to make disappear. Fat is the chief reason why people gain weight. So, if you wish to become lighter and look better, if you wish to achieve optimal health, you must get rid not of water but of fat.

The BHMD helps restore your figure by the philosophy that when weight is to be lost rapidly, eating all the more must be made a delight. That's why you have been given menus to please and thrill you day after day, week after week. Picking and choosing from the BHMD culinary selections will become an enjoyable part of your daily routine.

The components of the BHMD are those which God has diffused through nature for your wellbeing. I do not look upon the dieter as a "fat-burning" machine." I regard the human body as a temple whose organs and processes must be treated with respect. Short and deceptive dietary rituals will not help maintain the body. With their invocation, the temple will collapse. On the BHMD fat is lost without disturbing the sacred vessels of your organism.

Complex Carbohydrates are the main fare of the BHMD. They help melt fat away in a way that is Simple, Safe, and Speedy. If you stick to C.C., the effects are permanent. And it may add years to your life.

LET'S ACT LIKE GROWNUPS

When we talk about diets there is no point in fooling ourselves. The Beverly Hills Medical Diet is no pacifier to still your anxieties about weight. It is no fairy tale in which a wand waves and fat drops automatically. This is what the BHMD *will* do:

It tells you how to lose weight rapidly. Why you lose it. And what the diet contains that makes it work.

Certain kinds of diet books get my goat. They are the ones written as if the reader is a child who needs to be coaxed to reduce. This approach is not the least irritating quality of the Scarsdale diet, in which the hazardous ketone-stimulated water loss is justified by the rationale that the dieter needs to see immediate results. This type of "evidence," so goes the claim, will encourage the dieter through reinforcement to persist in his regimen.

Such reasoning is hardly the approach to a successful, life-time diet. The BHMD reshapes your eating habits because it is in your pattern of food consumption that weight was gained in the first place. The BHMD adjusts your fat person's body to that of a slender person, who will stay slender permanently. The high-protein dieter who has been turned into a nervous "sprinkler" is essentially still as fat as he was before. As you will learn after sampling the delicious BHMD menus, there is a difference between weight loss and fat loss.

During my medical-nutritional seminars at the American Institute of Health, I try to involve my patients more deeply into the question of their health. I explain that being merely the guardian of their medical data, it really doesn't belong to me. It is theirs and they are the ones who should be concerned about it. Thus they are motivated to do what they know they should be doing anyway. We are partners, I explain, but they are the senior partners in our program of nutrition and stress management.

13

There are hundreds of medical tricks that would enable me to delude their trust. But I believe in treating the dieter as an adult capable of taking responsibility in his own hands.

With the same frankness I confront the apology made for ketosis. An increase of ketone bodies in the blood is said to curb appetite. I consider such panaceas unnecessary, especially when they are the result of the real dangers posed by ketones. The BHMD has the best appetite restrainer in the world. That is the feeling of being full. The greater amount of chewing required by the C.C. diet, with the subsequent increase of saliva and gastric juices, gives the stomach a sated and satisfied feeling.

Dieting requires a certain amount of discipline. I recognize that voluntary restraint is not an easy matter. With the BHMD, however, this kind of self-control is made a cinch.

CHAPTER THREE:

WHY THE BHMD IS THE BEST DIET FOR YOU

HAZARDS OF KETOSIS

I would not feel so strongly about the low-carbohydrate/high-protein diet if it were not for the bodily harm it's known to create. Among the least alarming side effects are calcium depletion, dehydration, sleeplessness, nausea and fatigue.

Quite serious is the damage ketosis may cause for people with kidney problems.

And most serious is the linkage between ketone-producing high-protein, high-fat diets and atherosclerosis, gout, hypoglycemia, vascular thrombosis, liver and gall bladder diseases, hypertension, cancer of the colon and breast, cardiac arrhythmias, postural hypotension and coronary heart disease.

I've purposely put the risk elements of the low-carbohydrate/high-protein diet in a row. I *did* mean to scare you.

STOP KILLING YOURSELF

Sometimes shock is the only thing that will bring home a point. In my practice and in my mini-clinics in Beverly Hills I've often judged it necessary to resort to such blunt tactics to make people care. The dietary facts sometimes need to seize people by the throat and give them a good shaking to make them realize what they are doing to themselves by their overweight and destructive eating practices.

I've actually found an element of fatalism in the recklessness with which we Americans eat, smoke, drink and diet.

Perhaps that's because it's now commonplace to spend the last twenty years of our lives under a cardiologist's supervision. Perhaps it's rather ordinary for someone you know to have had by-pass surgery. Perhaps we figure we're all going to get cancer sooner or later anyway. Perhaps there is an unconscious fear that the whole world is going to blow up and that we may as well begin with ourselves.

Whatever the reason may be, I've found that there is a connection between these fatalistic attitudes and the fact that the average American is fat, that he has a cholesterol level of over 230, and that he will spend the remaining two decades of his life being treated for one thing after another.

It is due to nonchalance about the way you eat and about your body that you have a one-in-three chance of dying of a heart attack by age 60. Your condition is critical enough for the time to have come that no diet can be complete without dealing with the stress factor. Stress, overweight and faulty eating practices almost ensure that you may never reach old age.

The BHMD can preserve you from this fate. It can stop the breakneck pace at which you are wrecking your health and gambling with the chances of longevity. The BHMD provides a fast and simple program to defeat our grim nutritional statistics.

If you are too heavy and do not exercise your body, the BHMD tells you which foods you should be eating to bring down your weight. If you smoke and drink alcohol, you must stop, or at least cut down to the absolute minimum. The BHMD literally urges you to "take your heart for a walk." And it stipulates that *you must begin by replacing fatty and oily foods with others rich in Complex Carbohydrates.*

That's because C.C. provides the best, the fastest and safest way to lose weight without the hazards of ketosis

DANGERS OF OTHER DIETS

The high-protein/low-carbohydrate diet also causes other problems, one of which is bone loss. Osteoporosis, which is thinning of the bone due to calcium loss, is getting to be fairly common in our society. By the time we turn fifty we

16

can start to see significant bone loss on X-ray. Our bones thin out causing more bone breaks (fractures) as well as actual loss in height due to thinning and collapse of vertebrae.

This comes about because a high-protein diet increases calcium loss in the urine. In addition, the excess nitrogen and sulfur from the proteins in the blood are acid by-products of protein metabolism. The acidity literally leaches the calcium out of the bone.

What happens is that a state of negative calcium balance is produced. It means the body is losing more calcium than it is taking in. Adding calcium to our foods or in supplements does not seem to help reverse the negative calcium balance and protect bones against more osteoporosis. Getting off the high-protein diet *does,* however, cause the calcium balance to become positive, i.e., more calcium enters than is lost.

The average American is getting too many of his daily calories in protein. This means that he is risking the loss of the important mineral calcium. As a result he is susceptible to spontaneous bone fractures and loss of height, both due to thinning of bone.

In addition, other valuable minerals are lost, including zinc, iron and magnesium. We pay for this in our middle age.

HOW DOES KETOSIS WORK?

The sensible nutrition of the BHMD reflects a way of eating that you can live with day in and day out. It helps avoid the disastrous illnesses and potential deaths that may occur with some of the other diets, such as those featuring high-protein/low-carbohydrate.

The "other" diets take different forms. They continually pop up in new guises.

The so-called "protein-sparing modified fast" swept the country about four years ago. It is still around as the protein powder diet.

The protein powder taken by mouth, so goes the theory, prevents the body from breaking down its own protein in the form of muscles, heart, lungs, liver, skin, etc. Consequently, only fat would be burned for fuel for the body in the absence of carbohydrates. So many of the young nurses at the hospitals I attended used these diets and so many of them had multiple symptoms of dizziness, weakness, fainting and shriveling of skin that I was forced to study this ill-fated program in order to help them see the bad side effects.

In 1979, reports of deaths associated with the diet appeared first in the prestigious New England Journal of Medicine. Autopsy studies of the people on this diet – usually young women – showed breakdown of the very protein tissues (heart, liver and others) this diet was supposed to protect.

It turned out that the theory was wrong. The body cannot utilize protein in this or any other diet without carbohydrates. Actually, it is really the carbohydrates which protect the protein tissues from undergoing degeneration.

Then, why did people want to use the high-protein diet? Did it cause a fast weight loss? Yes it did, and still does. But the weight loss is not fat loss. It is fluid, that is, water loss.

The reason is simple. All this excess protein that is taken in must be metabolized, and protein requires *seven* times as much water for its metabolism as Complex Carbohydrates do. The major mode of excretion of metabolized protein is in the urine, much of it as urea (the substance that imparts the characteristic yellow color to the urine). So it takes lots and lots of water to cause this protein excretion. This weight loss is quickly regained.

After 1½ to 2 days on the high protein diet the glycogen (carbohydrate stored in muscles) is exhausted and the great weight loss occurs. This is the salt-linked carbohydrate fluid loss – a large loss of fluid and minerals in the urine. The great fatigue which occurs at this point reflects the water and mineral losses which grow worse as the days progress.

The claim is made that at this point the body will start producing ketones and that then the fat will melt away. The ketones, as you have learned, are breakdown products of fats – incompletely metabolized fats. When fat is completely metabolized no ketosis occurs since the fat is broken down completely.

When ketosis occurs in people with diabetes mellitus it heralds a rather severe situation as this represents an abnormal demand upon the body. Large amounts of ketones in diabetes can help cause the so-called diabetic coma.

In the non-diabetic at the very least it can cause damaged body chemistry, as well as mineral and vitamin losses. As ketones are being formed and being excreted the body's defense against illness, the immune system, suffers. Sensitivity to cold occurs. The thyroid hormone decreases. Changes-for-the-worse show up in liver tests. The blood uric acid increases and this may precipitate a fullblown gout attack.

Further deteriorations become prominent, such as a decrease in blood volume, which may lead to postural hypotension. This is a drop in blood pressure upon standing, leading to dizziness and weakness. Changes-for-the-worse occur in the ability of the kidneys to excrete waste material. The large potassium loss has been well documented, and I have seen patients on this diet brought to the hospital because of heart irregularities.

Hyponatremia, which is a sodium loss to a degree which is unhealthy, may occur and often is responsible for nausea, vomiting, dizziness, and apathy.

Magnesium and calcium losses occur in gradually diminishing amounts and the effect on the body, especially on the heart and nervous system, can be bad.

A drastic weight reduction program such as the high-protein, low-carbohydrate diet can cause a flattening of the lining of the intestine and can interfere with absorption of nutrients, causing what we call a malabsorption syndrome.

Vitamin deficiencies also occur in this type of diet. While ingesting protein liquid or powder, the amount of B-vitamins excreted in the urine exceeds that of the healthy individual.

AN END TO DIETARY HORROR

I could go on and on about the dangerous aspects of this fad diet or any other fad diet. The high-protein/high-fat/low-carbohydrate diet presents to me a horror story of grisly proportions. Fortunately, it has been my pleasure to put an end to its hazardous workings for a number of people.

I have seen many people who were once advocates of the high-protein diet. One of these was BJ, a 40-year-old woman who attended a university-sponsored high-protein diet program for eight months and lost 80 pounds. Her scalp hair thinned out, she was "cold all the time", felt weak, was dizzy, had dry skin, etc. She gained all of her weight back plus 10 pounds. She had more illness during and after the diet than she had before.

CHAPTER FOUR:

THE ELEMENTS OF THE BHMD

HIDDEN FATS & CHOLESTEROL

In my quick review of how the low-carbohydrate/high-protein diets put you in harm's way, it's well to remember two medical prefixes, neither of which mean much good: they are *hyper* and *hypo*. *Hyper* means "overactive": *hypo* means "underactive."

A diet that is very low in carbohydrates and high in protein is usually rich in fat and low in fiber. Many cholesterols and fats are hidden in what we think are high-protein foods, such as beef or cheese. Fat-rich foods, in turn, are linked to high levels of blood cholesterol and to compounds known as triglycerides, which put free fatty acids in your blood.

Now, for some jawbreakers: *hyperlipidemia* (lipids are fats), *hypercholesterolemia* and *hypertriglyceridemia* are associated with coronary heart disease and atherosclerosis. *Hyperuricemia* means a significant increase in uric acid in the blood, which can promote gout.

All these "overactive" processes are spurred by the ketone-production of diets with low-carbohydrate and high-protein content.

As for the "underactive" effects of such diets, *hypoglycemia* means insufficient blood sugar; postural *hypotension* means the trouble you may experience raising yourself up from a supine position.

Common among dieters is the idea that if they but switch from fats and oils to the high-protein diet, as recommended by Scarsdale, Atkins, *et al,* the cholesterol issue is dealt with. For example, they are apt to go along with a diet that allows an abundance of lean meat (beef, lamb, veal); chicken and turkey (with skin removed); lean fish (perch, flounder, haddock, cod); hard-boiled eggs, and cheese.

However, a diet of this sort is virtually restricted to protein and fat. As such it is a mine field seeded with ketosis.

The BHMD has a different approach. It considers all fats equally bad. It also tells you not to get caught up counting cholesterol, or worrying about polyunsaturated, saturated and unsaturated fats. The average American gets 40 to 50% of his calories from fats. The figure should be down to about 20%, and on the BHMD it is actually lower.

It has already been stated that the BHMD is thumbs down on all unnecessary fats. To be on the safe side allow me to add that the same goes for the unsaturated vegetable oils. They are merely vegetable fat which has been processed out of the vegetable. In the vegetable the oil is part of its natural container and harmless. But once it has been passed into an artificial container like a bottle it's another matter entirely.

C.C. vs. FATS & OILS

In the BHMD fats and oils are replaced by Complex Carbohydrates. These will make you lose weight and in addition do something even more beneficial. As part of your daily diet, C.C. protects you against heart disease and cancer.

The Complex Carbohydrates keep your arteries from clogging up with fats that slow down the flow of blood. For it is one of those marvels of nature that Complex Carbohydrates have the fantastic effect of *lowering* blood cholesterol. Thus, among its many other wonders, C.C. reduces the risk of coronary attacks.

A good deal of the Complex Carbohydrates that will buoy up your new diet will be consumed as fiber. The popular high-protein diets are almost criminally deficient in the all-important roughage that comes from the indigestible parts of fruits, vegetables, cereals and grains. Fiber, or "bulk," is incorporated as many delicious items in the BHMD.

And for a very good reason.

It has been shown scientifically that fiber helps increase the body's excretion of cholesterol. With the C.C.-rich fiber you are gaining greater protection against cancer of the colon and the rectum, the most prevalent forms of lethal cancer in our country.

The BHMD offers a wide and zesty assortment of snacks, meals and dishes to reduce your fat intake. For now, let's take one example: the simple potato.

Most people believe that a diet of lean meat will get your weight down better than a diet containing potatoes. But a 3½-oz. porterhouse steak is 82% fat and counts 465 calories. A 3½-oz. baked potato, however, contains only 93 calories and is only 0.5% fat. Compare this to a hot dog (80% fat); lunch meat (84%); peanut butter (77%); or take the average cheeseburger, in which the meat is 85% fat, the cheese is 73% fat, and the sauce is 90% fat.

The proof is in the potato, as your scale will verify.

DON'T EAT FOODS HIGH IN CHOLESTEROL

There are two kinds of cholesterol you should be concerned with. HDL (High Density Lipoprotein) and LDL (Low Density Lipoprotein), known as the good and bad cholesterol, respectively.

Lipoproteins exist to carry fats through your bloodstream, which is a watery medium. LDL can be characterized as a delivery truck, despositing fats into your cells, and clogging up your arteries. HDL is a scavenger, gathering up fats and cholesterol; in effect, cleaning up your arteries.

Thus, while your overall cholesterol should be low (below 180), you should also be concerned with the ratio of HDL to total cholesterol.

Here is how you can perform your own coronary risk factor test: Divide total cholesterol by HDL:

$$\frac{\text{total cholesterol}}{\text{HDL}}$$

The lower the figure, the better. A ratio of 3.5 is what you want. A ratio between 7 and 9 doubles the standard risk of a heart attack, and a ratio above 12 or 13 indicates a 300% greater chance of suffering heart disease. (Ask your doctor for HDL reading).

CARBOHYDRATES: REFINED AND UNREFINED

So far we've focused on the "good" carbohydrate, the C.C. But in the drama of dining there is also a "villain" carbohydrate. This element is all the more treacherous because it comes in a sweet, easily digestible and tempting form. It is the *refined carbohydrate*.

The chief culprit of the refined carbohydrates is in that doughnut you're eating. It's sugar.

Here's how sugar goes to work: Once you have eaten the doughnut, the sugar it contains causes your blood sugar to rise sharply. Your body responds by having the pancreas pump out insulin to drive the blood sugar down. In turn, the adrenal glands go to work, attempting to stabilize the blood sugar by pouring out adrenal hormones.

Thus, what started with a simple sugary doughnut has resulted in a stress reaction. Eating that doughnut has forced your body to suffer through drastic changes in blood sugar. As a result, your body is tense and you are nervous.

Of course, your body can easily deal with the stress caused by one doughnut. It can maybe even deal with 1,000 doughnuts. But assaulted by demands to handle doughnuts, sugars, fats, salts, food additives, etc., your body will be overwhelmed and sooner or later it will give up.

Stressing your body to deal with harmful materials will result in a general breakdown of parts. Sugar is a refined carbohydrate that plays a big role in such stress. And that means *all* sugar. Whether it be brown, "raw," molasses, or in the form of honey.

We consume 128 pounds of sugar per person a year. But this astonishing amount does nothing for us. Our bodies do not benefit in the slightest. Sugar supplies neither protein, vitamins or minerals. As I tell my patients, sugar is a taker, not a giver. Sugar robs you of phosphorus, the B vitamin complex and magnesium. These important vitamins and minerals are used up in the metabolism of sugar.

The BHMD bans sugar because it makes you fat. I designed the BHMD to make you lose weight rapidly and to keep you slim for the rest of your life. But the diet is equally meant to maintain your health, to reduce stress, and make you live longer.

Sugar is the enemy of these noble aims. It is implicated in diabetes, heart disease, elevated blood cholesterol and serum triglyceride levels, mental problems, tooth decay, dermatitis, and high blood pressure.

My diet deals with the sugar issue by having you feast on a variety of starch-rich foods filled with naturally occurring sugar. Complex Carbohydrates like fruits, vegetables, grains, peas and lentils, are what nature designed you to function on. The BHMD offers them in such a luscious and exotic variety that you will *not want to* add sugar to your daily meals.

NO MORE 'SUGAR RUSH'

Much of our sugar addiction is the result of the "sugar rush" that comes from eating refined sugar. A simple carbohydrate such as sugar throws 50 to 100 calories into your bloodstream at one time. This "rush" causes these simple sugars to burn up too rapidly, triggering hypoglycemia, which means low blood sugar. This condition signals the brain to crave more sugars, thus stimulating appetite.

On the other hand, the unrefined Complex Carbohydrate, such as starch, enter the blood stream evenly. It burns up completely and in this slow process a steady, balanced and leisurely supply of sugar is fed to the blood. Consequently, it eliminates the "appetite swings" commonly experienced by people with high sugar intake.

Low blood sugar that results in a craving for more sugar is perhaps one of the more obnoxious effects of the high-protein diets. It is probably a factor in the disappointing record of those who have tried these regimen.

It is remarkable that hypoglycemia, that is low blood sugar, is virtually absent in parts of the world where the diet consists of Complex Carbohydrates.

Though the popular high-protein diets recognize, like all diets, the harm of refined sugar, they get around the problem by something even more questionable. That is, artificial sweeteners. The BHMD frowns on the use of all chemicals and food additives. The effect such substances as saccharine appears to have on cancer incidence is too alarming for comfort.

On the BHMD you learn to like sugar in the form nature intended you to have it. Coupled to your joy of quick weight loss will be the relief of bringing your appetite under control. And this wonder will come about without the dangerous side effect of artificial sugar substitutes.

HALT TO SALT

The biggest dietary myth next to protein concerns salt.

Somehow, people believe they need salt. So the average person sprinkles it on his food as if he is doing his body a favor. Many athletes are still convinced that

24

perspiring causes the body to need more salt—when in actual fact all the body requires is more water. Food manufacturers pour salt on their products in the belief that they are pleasing consumers. As a result the average person eats far more salt than he should, sometimes as much as 20 times more than needed.

But did you know? You *do not* need salt at all! In fact, if you're anything like the average American salt is probably killing you.

What you *do* need is sodium. A normal individual requires about 400 mgs. of sodium per day. Table salt is 40% sodium. Your daily need does not exceed more than 1/20 teaspoon, and by eating almost any unsalted food you will more than meet this requirement.

In the BHMD I make a distinction: Salt is what you *add* to food. Sodium is what is already *in* the food.

If you have a "salty" tooth, the BHMD furnishes enough natural salts in its C.C.-rich menus to satisfy your tastes. You can choose from a tempting variety of gourmet delights and exciting dishes seasoned with flavors from herbs, spices and natural condiments. Through such "salt-ernatives" you will never more reach for the shaker.

I am very serious about reducing your sodium intake for two reasons. Sodium is a retainer of water, and by cutting down on salt you will rapidly shed as much as five pounds. Your body stores this water to dilute the sodium, and with less sodium less water needs to be retained.

Secondly, sodium is a powerful stressor. If the body takes in too much sodium it can take the kidneys up to 48 hours to eliminate the excess. Overloaded with sodium, water flows from the cells into the fluid surrounding them. Then it passes into the blood, and this is what gives some overweight people a bloated look as well as a bloated feeling.

Robbed of their water the cells function less efficiently. But that is not all.

Retention of water leads to high blood pressure and its associated diseases. As the tissues are flooded your heart has to pump harder. The heart literally has to drain a waterlogged body. These pressures contribute to headaches, congestive heart failure, depression, pre-menstrual tensions, migraine, and that most serious stress condition of all, hypertension.

In northern Japan, hypertension is a leading cause of death. The people there eat about 40,000 mgs. of salt a day!

On the BHMD you reform your eating habits in order that your lost weight will stay lost. The high-protein diets with their limited variety of tastes and flavors cannot adequately reform your ingrained disposition for harmful substances. Scarsdale and Atkins perpetuate the unwholesome cravings for sugar and salt. Furthermore, because they contain too much fats and cholesterols and too little Complex Carbohydrates, they maximize the causes of hypertension. With 20% of Americans prone to this stressful disorder, it is a very grave shortcoming, indeed.

While you follow the BHMD your craving for salt diminishes. That is because the diet makes abundant provision for tasty combinations. It has recipes from all over the world in which the salt flavors are part of the natural ingredients.

VITAMINS & MINERALS

If you were living in an optimal environment where the air and soil were pure and the food came to you in its unblemished, untampered, virgin condition, then I would say, you don't need vitamins and minerals. But look at the facts.

The nutritive value of many of our foods is destroyed before it reaches the consumer. Our fruits and vegetables look beautiful, but they are not especially wholesome. Our food processors perform all kinds of wizardry, as the sweetened, homogenized, stabilized, anti-oxidated, chelated, anticaked, firmed, softened and flavored products on our shelves testify.

How a typical frozen pizza is made

You start with wheat, corn, soybeans, and sugar cane. The wheat is stripped of all its nutritive value, and made into refined flour. Oxidation agents are added to make the refined flour into stiffened gluten flour.

The corn is crushed into refined starch, 'cross-linking agents' are added to make the refined starch into modified starch.

The soybeans are converted to protein flour and oil.

The protein flour is extruded and refined into textured vegetable protein.

The oil is hydrogenated into margarine.

The sugar cane is made into raw sugar, and then refined into refined sugar.

The stiffened gluten flour, modified starch, textured vegetable protein, margarine and refined sugar are emulsified, acidulated, conditioned, synthetically dyed, artificially flavored, etc., into artificial cheese, artificial tomato, simulated Italian sausage, and the pizza shell.

We do not eat properly. Our average diet favors meat and other high-protein substances. These are deficient in Vitamin E, the B complex, Vitamin C, zinc, calcium, magnesium, and a host of other necessary nutrients.

At home and in our restaurants we broil, roast, toast and bake the last shred of nutritive value from our food. Our vegetables are soggy. The grains we eat have actually "massacred" legions of rats. Our fruit juices, with all the bulk removed, are nothing but the color and the sugar.

Besides the sorry state of our food and the way we prepare it, other factors deprive you of valuable nutrients. Common drugs such as aspirin, birth control pills, antacids and antibiotics interefere with vitamin and mineral uptake.

In addition, there are things we cannot control, though they impose increased nutritive demands, e.g., air and water pollution, smoking, alcohol, stress.

But not only does our life style diminish our supply of essential nutrients. The "refined" or processed foods we eat are stealthy burglars that "rob" you of the vitamins and minerals you *do* have. A serious lack of these may lead to every kind of ailment, from loose gums to breakdown of important organs and, ultimately, death.

I give all my patients a Mineral Analysis and Dietary Survey. I have yet to find a patient with the proper amount and balance of vitamins and nutrients.

Losing weight in a rapid and efficient manner is an absolute certainty if you follow the BHMD. But it is just as important that you feel healthy, vibrant — *alive!* Your environment and the way you live conspire to deprive you of the nutrients essential to your wellbeing. Therefore, the BHMD subscribes to supplements of vitamins and minerals. As a doctor I can't recommend vita- mins and minerals for you individually. In the *Stress* chapter, however, I explain the usefulness of vitamin and mineral supplements and how, after consultation with your physician, they can work for you.

C.C.: THE ENERGIZER

I shall bid adieu to my pet peeve, the high-protein diets as trumpeted by the false prophets with a final remark about fatigue.

My point will be illustrated by a study that was done with respect to a low-carbohydrate diet on some troops in the Canadian Army during World War II. In that study, the predictable effects of ketosis were made immediately apparent. An unsoldierly group of weary, listless men with sunken eyes emerged from four days of this diet. In their dehydrated and exhausted condition they showed dramatically the results of a regimen free from Complex Carbohydrates.

27

In the experiment the troops had been given pemmican to eat. The idea was that pemmican – a high-protein dried beef with suet – might be used as a highly-concentrated, high-energy source. With the pemmican they were given tea to drink.

The distressing results surprised the Army medics. Within three days the men were unable to function normally. They were nauseaous, some vomited, all were incapacitated by fatigue. They had no appetite and because of great water loss they had the *appearance* of having lost considerable weight.

Only when the men were returned to rations with sufficient carbohydrate did the fatigue and nausea disappear.

The same symptomatic lack of physical energy was reported in another experiment with low-carbohydrate diets conducted in the United States. Again, the fatigue vanished miraculously after carbohydrate was restored to the diet.

Today we know that the fatigue, dizziness and headaches experienced by people on the popular but perilous high-protein prescriptions are caused by the "after-burn" of excessive protein. Unable to synthesize adequate amounts of glucose (blood sugar) on high-protein regimen, the body is forced to break down its own muscle and tissue proteins to get glucose. The sluggishness, dizziness and fatigue occur because due to insufficient C.C., not enough glucose (the brain's main fuel) reaches the brain.

BHMD IS NOT VEGETARIAN

The BHMD supplies all the fats and protein your body needs. The ingredients and condiments that make up the appetizing BHMD menus provide your body with the essentials of protein. These basic building blocks of the body, you may recall, are *amino acids*.

The amino acids, not the protein, are important for your body's vital metabolic functions. As part of the C.C., the amino acids perform their jobs with a far greater efficiency than the protein derived from meats.

However, that is not to say that the BHMD is a vegetarian diet. Your menus make plenty of allowance to indulge your taste for animal substances. Various types of lean meats, chicken and other poultry, as well as fish are included in the C.C. fare. You will prepare them in a way that permits you to obtain the greatest benefit from them. Nevertheless, the daily quantity should not exceed more than a quarter pound.

CHAPTER FIVE:

THE BHMD WAY TO STRESS-FREE EATING

WHAT IS STRESS?

Of the ten leading causes of death in this country today, eight are in some way related to stress. Such an alarming statistic is apt to contribute to more stress. But with the BHMD you can do something about it.

The BHMD cannot make your life totally stress-free. There are other factors in your life, environmental, personal, etc., which do not touch upon the question of weight loss and diet. Two elements of stress, however, the BHMD *can* take out of your life. These two are associated with many of the diseases that cut down the life span. They are also responsible for overweight, as well as the "roller-coaster" effect of other diets.

First there is the stress caused by the lowered self-esteem and self-confidence due to being overweight. This type of stress works on the psychological level. It keeps the dieter confined to a vicious circle. The poor self-image many overweight persons have keeps them from losing weight because of "nervous eating."

A second and very important cause of stress has to do directly with nutrition. We know that fighting your spouse is stress. Getting mad because you are stuck in traffic is stress. Working harder than you are able to is stress. But you may not realize that eating a candy bar or Big Mac is stress.

29

I define stress as *the non-specific response of the body, mind or emotions to any demand made upon them.*

In terms of nutrition the response primarily involves the body. But we should not underestimate the emotional component. We already saw how through lowered self-esteem a person anxious to lose weight defeats his goal through "nervous eating."

Any time you ask your body to respond to something, whether it be physical or emotional, you are stressing your body. Let's see what I mean by looking at the Big Mac you just consumed.

Your unwise choice for lunch has caused stress on two levels:

1) With your burger came the sting of conscience for eating something fattening. The Big Mac created guilt feelings. That's emotional stress.

2) By demolishing the hefty burger you pitted your body against an invasion of 1,510 mgs. of sodium, or four times your daily requirement. Counting the salt in the pickle, mustard and ketchup, you consumed with the Big Mac a total of 2,091 mgs. salt, or seven times what you need for the day.

This intake of salt puts tremendous stress on your chemical and cellular levels. Salt, like sugar, fats and additives chemically harm the body. It puts an extra strain on your heart. It is liable to cause hypertension. Salt can affect your kidneys and blood pressure in a very unpleasant way. Salt is a stressor, and any kind of stress crimps your determination to stay on the diet and lose weight fast.

EVALUATE YOUR STRESS

The *Self-Evaluation* list identifies the various ways that stress evidences itself in your life. It is graded on a 1 to 4 basis. Too many 3s or 4s should serve to warn you that an illness may be on the way if stress is not properly handled.

Many symptoms may be related to the effects of stress. Mark according to the accompanying scale the frequency with which you have had the following symptoms in the past three months.

1. *I haven't had the problem.*
2. *Occasionally.*
3. *Frequently.*
4. *Nearly all the time or constant.*

1. Aches (neck & shoulders)_____
2. Alcohol usage _____
3. Allergy problems _____
4. Angry feelings _____
5. Arthritis _____
6. Asthma attacks _____
7. Cold hands & feet _____
8. Colitis attacks _____
9. Common cold _____
10. Common flu _____
11. Constipation _____
12. Depression _____
13. Dermatitis _____
14. Diarrhea _____
15. Early morning awakenings _____
16. Fatigue _____
17. Heart palpitations _____
18. Headaches (tension) _____
19. High blood pressure _____
20. Hives _____
21. Hyperventilation _____
23. Infections, low grade _____
24. Indigestion _____
25. Loss of appetite _____
26. Low back pains _____
27. Menstrual distress _____
28. Migraine headaches _____
29. Minor illnesses _____
30. Nausea _____
31. Nervous feelings _____
32. Nightmares _____
33. Non-prescription drugs _____
34. Overeating _____
35. Peptic ulcer _____
36. Prescription drug use _____
37. Sexual problems _____
38. Sleep-onset insomnia_____
39. Vomiting _____
40. Worrying thoughts _____
41. Others _____

STRESS AND YOUR CHEMISTRY

Of the many stress factors that assault you, the BHMD is concerned primarily with those affecting nutrition. Moreover, it looks at them in the main on how they interfere with successful weight loss. The BHMD holds to the premise that once the stress-producing elements have been removed from the foods you eat all the rest will be made easier.

Without stress your weight loss is facilitated. With the emergence of a slimmer, healthier, more attractive you, self-esteem and self-confidence return. With the positive reactions to your more appealing appearance you are further encouraged to stay on the diet. In turn, self-approval is reinforced. And thus it goes, one positive factor reinforcing another until the diet's goal has been achieved: the full integration of your physical and psychological wellbeing through rapid, simple — and *enjoyable!* — weight reduction.

To obtain this optimum state of rapid and permanent weight loss together with a relaxed mental condition the BHMD begins by changing your food intake. Scientists are now coming to believe that much of our behavior is influenced by the body's chemistry. Quite a number of them are inclined to see stress as an important factor in altering that chemistry. And since the body's chemistry is affected by diet, there is a growing readiness to combat stress through the right kind of nutrition. The "nervous eater" frequently reacts not so much to his craving for food as to the stress built up in his body through faulty eating practices.

To illustrate, here's a typical question I'm asked in my practice and health seminars: "Is there any harm in drinking lots of Diet Pepsi to cut down my appetite, Dr. Fox?"

A question of this nature usually leads to a discussion of the role of food stressors and how they frustrate the rapid weight-loss process.

I begin by pointing out the health hazards. I explain that the various diet colas are destructive to the immune system by tearing into the body with a huge chemical load. Our immune system repels foreign invaders such as bacteria, viruses and cancer cells. The continual stress caused by food additives and chemicals result in a devastated immune system. Through this ravaged barrier, it is held, enter the conditions producing cancer and other serious illnesses.

But food stressors not only cut down the chances for health and longevity. If it is your object to slim and stay slim, they are the gremlins that play hob with your good intentions. Simply put, food stressors interfere with discipline.

You have already seen how the doughnut sets off severe blood sugar fluctuations. The sugar in the doughnut drives up your blood sugar and throws the adrenal hormones into a tailspin. Dietwise, it tends to make you lose control of your appetite regulation. Sugar is a stressor. Stress makes you tense. It makes you nervous. Because you are tense and nervous you are not in the proper frame to maintain your diet. Only by eliminating nutritional stress can you prevent your appetite from running wild. And you'll be surprised to find how easily that can be accomplished.

For it is one of the virtues of the BHMD that while you lose weight your tastes undergo a permanent change. Instead of refined sugars, you savor the "hidden" sugars in starches and legumes. Instead of salt, you want the natural tartness of certain grains and vegetables, or the seasonings on lean meats. Instead of reaching for a diet cola, you find yourself asking for a glass of water, mineral, sparkling, or plain, with a slice of lemon.

The BHMD offers a large selection of natural and tasty suggestions to replace your old fattening and destructive eating habits. In the process your deadened taste buds spring alive again. A whole new world of flavors and savors is opened up to you. And almost without realizing it, you become a disciplined eater.

BELLING THE 'CAT'

The sugars, fats and salts, the additives and chemicals of processed foods, the excessive high-protein intake — all are stressors preventing the body from achieving the dietary balance which alone assures permanent weight loss. But thus far I've said little about some of the most powerful stressors. I call them by a compound name, CAT—that is, Coffee, Alcohol and Tobacco.

All three are stressors which have no place in a complete and healthful diet. I believe enough is known about their dangers to your health without another exposition of their alarming effects. As far as tobacco is concerned, just consult the warning on a cigarette pack. The immoderate use of coffee and alcohol provides another list of grisly medical facts. Suffice it to say that in combination with a high-protein diet the effects of CAT over an extended period of time are suicidal.

The BHMD, though recognizing the dangers of CAT, has a different way of tackling the monster. It is a step-by-step approach rather than a full, head-on attack. I believe that you will be better able to face the CAT after *first* having experienced your quick and easy weight loss.

It is here that I must profess my limitations. As a doctor I can only give the patient opinions. As far as diet is concerned, only the patient can really change his own life. I can tell a patient what's best for him, but only the patient can implement my advice. On the other hand, the serious dieter frequently is the best judge of his own capacity to follow the rules. Therefore, a patient may find it necessary, for example, to use salt in order to reduce his calorie intake while on my diet plan.

Although I know it's not the best way, I realize that it is better than the more serious danger of being overweight. Giant steps are better than small steps, but small steps are better than no steps at all.

However, once you have adjusted yourself to the BHMD it is more likely that you'll be like the runner who builds up stamina to stay the full course. When you look at your new figure you'll be brimming with renewed confidence and self-esteem. The discipline you have acquired almost effortlessly will encourage you to 'bell the CAT.'

REPLACING STRESS WITH ZEST

Unlike the other popular diets, the BHMD incorporates an anti-stress program. By habituating you to proper nutrition the BHMD reduces the stress which leads to heart disease and cancer. For this reason I call it a Long-Life Anti-Stress Program. The diet combats stress through a nutritional plan so composed that, ideally, 10% of your daily calories come from protein; 20% of your calories come from fat; and 70% of your calories come from Complex Carbohydrates.

Because the Complex Carbohydrates are much easier for your body to handle, they make less demand upon the organism. Consequently they create less stress, so that you'll feel more relaxed while dieting. In this painless manner you absorb the self-regulation and discipline almost unconsciously, making it a cinch to stick to your new, slim and healthful way of eating.

"I FEEL TEN YEARS LIGHTER"

The high-protein diets are an example of the narrow and short-sighted objective that seeks weight loss come hell or high water.

Stress is inseparable from the ketosis they produce, and stress is the reason they fail to maintain weight loss. High-protein diets actually build up *greater* stress, with the result that the Scarsdale plan, for instance, finds it necessary to admonish the dieter not to prolong the regimen beyond two weeks.

The BHMD has no need for such warnings. On the contrary, it tells you to diet and eat for the rest of your life. Because you love the succulent menus, your excess weight melts away in a jiffy. Because your tastebuds are revitalized, you want to eat no other way. The BHMD takes stress from your food and puts zest in your body. And because you feel good, you won't ever get back on the "roller-coaster" again.

I have had very great pleasure in seeing countless patients return to my office after a few weeks of dieting with trim new figures. But it has given me even more pleasure to see their energy and bounce and joy for life. They were no longer depressed or nervous. They looked better, they felt better. They had changed not just in appearance but in their unstressful inward selves. "Not only am I ten pounds lighter," one middle-aged lady reported to me with a glow, *"I feel ten years lighter."*

This same lady, incidentally, had gotten into the "baggie"habit. The "baggie" is a small and helpful accessory to the BHMD which helps you overcome the "munchies." Instead of reaching for a candy bar, you dip into a baggie containing an assortment of fresh vegetables and bite-size fruit slices. The baggie allows you to nibble all day while maintaining your fast weight reduction.

VITAMINS & MINERALS FOR STRESS

The BHMD makes your diet as rapid and painless as possible. Therefore, it eliminates all elements that may cause stress. The supplements of vitamins and minerals I recommend are to ensure that stress remains absent. Without stress you are at your peak mental and physical wellbeing. In that state your weight-shedding program is facilitated to the optimum degree.

I have already stated why I consider vitamin and mineral supplements advisable. Though the BHMD offers both a variety and proportion of foods that provide you with all the necessary nutrients, we simply cannot be certain that these nutrients are actually there by the time they reach your table. In the way our foods are grown and processed it is likely that at least some of their nutrient values have vanished on their way to the supermarket.

Similarly, our health is affected by the environmental pollutants we breathe in and absorb. You are getting aluminum in your body every time you use an underarm deodorant or an antacid. Because you are getting all sorts of stress, it is obvious that you need something to combat it. Vitamin and mineral supplements are the most reliable way of assuring this.

Stress may interfere with your weight loss by complicating your diet with external factors. I shall take one element -- lead -- to show you why I consider the vitamin and mineral supplements necessary.

How does lead get to you?

First, lead may reach you through what you eat. When tuna is canned, the lead levels in the tuna increase *4,000* times. Secondly, there is the lead from the gasoline fumes which you inhale every time you get on a busy highway or street. Thirdly, cigarette smokers have a higher blood lead level, which may be due to the use of lead arsenate sprays on the soils where tobacco is grown.

Though lead may be useful in your home plumbing, inside your bodily plumbing it is not a very pleasant substance. Lead is a metabolic poison which inhibits many enzyme systems in the body. It interferes with almost all life processes, especially the nervous system, blood and kidneys.

Lead shortens the life span of red blood cells, it has an adverse effect on the heart and endocrine systems, and small amounts of lead reduce the resistance of humans and animals to infection. Futhermore, there is no telling what other pollutants you may be exposed to. Each year scientists discover new poisons in our environment.

My experience with patients who have been exposed to low concentrations of lead over a long period of time shows them to have symptoms such as fatigue, weakness, vertigo, headaches and depression. It stands to reason that at the very least these symptoms may disrupt the successful following of your diet. In the case of lead, supplements of Vitamin C and B vitamins, as well as calcium, enhance your ability to resist its toxic effects, as well as its possible interference with your diet.

VITAMINS & MINERALS: HOW MUCH & WHEN

My treatment of stress includes Vitamins A, the B Complex, C, and E, as well as pantothenic acid and zinc.

- Anywhere between 10,000 and 25,000 units of Vitamin A a day is a good safe amount for the average person, even if he is taking a lot of Vitamin A in vegetables.

- Vitamin C is an especially useful supplement. A lack of Vitamin C diminishes your capacity to resist stress. Furthermore, as it is not toxic, you can take as much as you like; the excess is eliminated. Besides its antiviral and antibacterial action, Vitamin C raises the High Density Lipoprotein

(HDL), the "good cholesterol." It also combats poisons from the environment, such as mercury and lead.

- Vitamin E is very important. A minimum of 400 milligrams twice a day,
of the E alpha tocopherol, helps your body guard itself against the effects
of whatever polyunsaturated oils may slip through your dietary censorship.

- Of the B-complex, at least 50 milligrams a day of the major B's is
recommended.

- Zinc is especially beneficial for very active people. About 50 milligrams
of chelated zinc a day should be sufficient.

- Of pantothenic acid, I suggest a minimum of 250 to 500 milligrams a day.

It is important to remember, however, that with vitamins and minerals the
question is not merely of how much you take but of *how* and *when* as well.
For example, just taking zinc by itself may upset other ratios, the zinc-
copper ratio, etc. So whenever you're taking minerals there should be at
least a smattering of *all* the other vitamins and at least one multi-mineral.

You will get the most out of your minerals if you take them twice a day.
With chromium, for example, take it with breakfast in the morning and
again with the evening meal. The same goes for zinc. Calcium happens to be
better absorbed when you're lying down. So it is best taken at night, which
gives you the added benefit of relaxing you before sleep.

DIET, STRESS & SEX

I can think of no better way to demonstrate the relationship between your new
diet and sex than to cite the case history of one of my patients.

Mr. Simmons, as I shall call him, came to my office one day to see me about
losing weight and to complain about a decrease in sexual energy. Outwardly, he
was not at all dissimilar from the successful middle-aged men that fill our
executive ranks. He was 52 years old, stood close to six feet, and weighed 200
pounds. Like the average American, he'd been gaining about a pound a year
since his twenties. He was also very much like the average American of his age
in that he had an unhealthy, feckless and tired look.

After discussing his fatigue and nervousness he finally came around to the real
underlying problem. He hesitated to mention it outright. He said cautiously that
his sexual life was rather lax. He woke up tired and went to bed tired. He took a
number of prescription drugs for nervousness, including Valium and Dalmane.
The trouble was his inability to maintain an erection. He blamed it on general
fatigue.

37

It is part of my routine that my patients fill out an extensive medical history. The details Mr. Simmons provided concerning his eating habits were not unusual, and *that* precisely was the problem. The fatigue he complained of, his overweight and his sexual impairment, were the natural consequences of a diet riddled with high-protein and stress.

For breakfast Mr. Simmons had toast, coffee, eggs and sausage. His average lunch consisted of steak, french fries and pie. For dinner he had something on the order of meat, vegetables, and dessert. In between he snacked on lots of nuts, cheese, drinks and potato chips. He smoked 40 cigarettes a day, drank about 10 cups of coffee, and some six 4 oz. glasses of wine. He would, in addition, have some alcohol and beer during the week. He used about 16 teaspoons of sugar a day, and did not exercise at all.

I prescribed the BHMD, with its daily menu plan and exercise guide. He went along without a murmur. Then he asked about the prescription for his sexual troubles. I merely told him that after he had followed the diet and done the exercises for two weeks, I would speak to him about this specific complaint.

I could hear his voice boom as he entered my office two weeks later. "Doctor, you've done it!"

Mr. Simmons looked extraordinary. He was ten pounds lighter, his eyes looked brighter, he gave out an air of vitality and confidence.

The question of his sexual complaint never came up.

THE TEN COMMANDMENTS
OF THE ANTI-STRESS DIET

1. Follow the menu closely. Eat only the foods listed and don't substitute anything not on the menu.
2. Snack all day long, if you desire. Blunt your hunger from the list of unrestricted foods.
3. Drink a minimum of six glasses of water daily.
4. Minimize drinking of alcoholic beverages.
5. Allowable liquids in order of preference include: water, Linden tea, mineral water (with lemon, if desired).
6. Eat the vegetables without butter, margarine, or any dressings not specified. Use only the dressings specified or lemon and vinegar.
7. For chicken or turkey, remove the skin and all visible fat before cooking. For meat use only the leanest.
8. If you're not hungry, don't eat!
9. Snack from the unrestricted list, but quit eating as soon as you're comfortably full.
10. Carry a "baggie" with you to snack on between meals.

CHAPTER SIX:

THE WONDERFUL WORLD OF WOGGING

FOR PEOPLE WHO HATE TO EXERCISE

When my patients ask me what they should do for exercise I tell them to wog.

At first they believe they have heard amiss.

"What is that, doctor?"

"Wog," I say blandly. "W-O-G."

They soon learn what that strange activity is. And before you can say 'exercise,' they've become enthusiastic woggers.

Wogging is my term for an activity that combines the best of two worlds: walking and jogging. In conjunction with the BHMD, wogging removes pounds of fat from your body. Wogging not only keeps your new lines firm, but it makes you feel altogether wonderful. Moreover, when done on a regular and systematic basis, wogging will prolong your life by many years.

It is generally agreed that there is no better workout for your body (and your mind!) than walking. It is also believed that if there is one thing that beats walking it is jogging. But I have found that jogging is not for everyone. For every ten people who become fanatic joggers, there are a hundred who before long fall off. And when they stop jogging, they don't return to a less demanding routine. Usually they stop exercising completely.

What is it that makes some people zealous converts to jogging, while the majority makes a determined stab and soon drops out? I think it may have something to do with the 'loneliness-of-the-long-distance-runner.' Despite the mental and physical elixir jogging provides, it is a rather strenuous and monotonous routine. The iron-willed who jog in and out of season are to be commended. But most of us are of frailer clay. We like to do something that is both pleasurable and not *too* demanding.

The majority of dieters, I've found, hate to exercise. If you belong to this class, then wogging is the answer for you. If you do not, then just keep on jogging.

TAKE YOUR HEART FOR A WOG

Wogging is very simple, but care should be taken that the proportions of walking and jogging are balanced. The key to exercise is your heart. You want to raise its pumping capacity through sustained physical activity. You may do this merely by walking, but obviously you increase the heart's strength more by the greater exertion of jogging. Nevertheless, as the BHMD keeps you slim forever through the right diet, so it will keep you exercising if you do it in a painless and moderate fashion. Walk a bit, jog a bit. Alternate each by a few minutes. Wogging is fun. It is not meant to be tiring.

Before you start wogging, especially if you are over thirty, check with a physician. If there are no contraindications, begin your exercise plan by setting out a two-mile course. My patients all start on a minimum of 30 minutes of wogging, four days a week. You will know how fast to go, and you will learn whether to emphasize walking or jogging — your heart will tell you.

Since a good part of your exercise will be spent walking, you can make it more enjoyable by choosing an interesting route. Perhaps the reason some people find jogging "boring" is that it absorbs their total concentration: joggers usually have little eye for observation other than the road ahead. But in wogging the "scenery" of your route can be a pleasurable distraction during the walking spells of the exercise. As speed is not a factor, there is plenty of opportunity to take in the sights or chat with a wogging companion.

If you live in a city with parks, you may wish to plan different routes. One day you may want to take in something of nature, the next you may like to get the feel of the city.

About half the time I like to wog in nearby Rancho Park. I get there about 7 a.m. when the sun is rising. I usually have had a tiny bit of cereal, a few crackers or a small piece of fruit before I set out. You should never wog on an empty stomach. It can actually be dangerous.

I choose the early morning for wogging, though another good time is in the evening before supper. I like the start of the day because Rancho Park is quiet and wogging through the trees and grass is most relaxing. You will get to appreciate, as I do, that the thirty minutes spent wogging sets you up with vigor and energy for the entire day.

When I'm not wogging in the park, I wog through downtown Beverly Hills. Frequently some of my out-of-town patients are waiting in front of their hotels to wog with me. We follow a set route that takes us up Wilshire Boulevard, past the Brown Derby Restaurant, then north on Rodeo Drive. Usually my fellow woggers slow to a walk on this luxurious shopping street to cast a peek into the windows of Gucci's and Fred's. At Little Santa Monica Blvd., with the Hollywood Hills on our right, we wog west past Camden, turning left on Bedford Drive and passing Daniel's Restaurant. Then we continue to wog along "shrinks' row" (several buildings housing numerous psychiatrists), past my offices and on to the Ginger Man, a restaurant owned by Caroll O'Connor (Archie Bunker). Then we turn again back onto Wilshire.

One of the delights of wogging is the "breather" provided by each stretch of walking. My out-of-town patients pace themselves so they fall into a walk in places they like to look at more closely. They enjoy wogging in the home of the "beautiful people" and they like to slow down to glance at the fashionable wares in the windows of Neiman Marcus and I. Magnin's on Wilshire.

After leaving these tempting windows behind, we pick up speed again along Roxbury Drive and Linden. Finally, wogging north on Beverly Drive we slow to a walk while passing such landmarks as the Old World Restaurant, R.J.'s, the Red Onion, Nate and Al's, and Ah Fong. Then we complete the wog by returning to my patients' hotel.

I've gone somewhat elaborately into my wogging routine to show that the thought of exercise should not scare you. Wogging can be both pleasurable and a social activity. And the beauty of it is that while you're enjoying yourself, you are burning up fat, rejuvenating your body and clearing cobwebs from your mind.

THE FINER POINTS OF WOGGING

Wogging is a very simple way for everybody — regardless of age — to look and feel younger, to live a fuller and healthier life, to improve the temperament and to avoid depression. It is the perfect exercise to complement and speed up your weight reduction. A few pointers will enable you to get the most out of wogging.

Learn to take your own pulse. It is best to take the carotid pulse, especially thick chest-walled people (A). Or, palpate yourself at the radial artery (the wrist, B), or the temporal artery (in front of the ear, C). Count the beats for 6 seconds and multiply by 10 to get the pulse rate. The norm is 70-80 per minute.

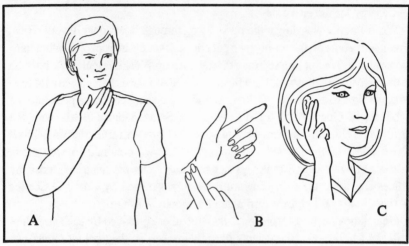

Next, there is an easy way to find out how much exercise is the right amount for you. While exercising, your heart should operate at a certain heartbeat capacity. After you've learned to take your pulse, figure out maximal attainable heart rate.

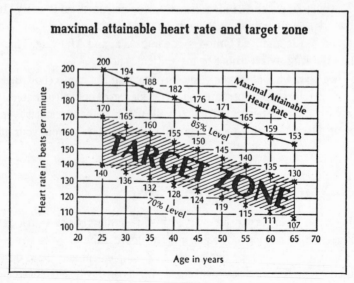

In order to benefit from exercise, you must raise your heart rate to 70% of its maximal attainable heart rate, and you must keep it there for about 30 minutes. For the vast majority of us, wogging is perfect. Activities such as tennis or football involve exertion, and do raise your heart rate, but only sporadically and in bursts. You want your heart to beat steadily at the 70% level.

To determine your 70% level, find on the chart the age in years closest to yours and read the number at the 70% level. For a fifty-year-old the 70% level is 119. Round that off to 120 and you're all set.

When you wog you're not concerned with how far you're going, or how fast you're moving. You're only concerned with keeping your heart beat at the 70% level.

For some people a brisk walk will do. Start slow. Your purpose is to develop a lifelong exercise plan - not win a gold medal. After a few weeks you'll notice you're able to wog farther and/or faster. That means your heart has gotten stronger. When your heart is stronger, it will take more exertion to raise your heart rate to the 70% level. Now you emphasize the jogging part of wogging.

When you begin wogging, you might have to stop every five minutes or so to check your pulse. Find your pulse beat and count it for a six-second period. Multiply by 10. That is your heart rate. After a few days you'll know about how fast you should be wogging; only check your pulse when you finish wogging. Do so immediately, as your heart rate begins to slow down as soon as you stop exercising.

If your pulse is too slow, speed up a bit. If it's too fast, slow down. Remember, it doesn't matter how far or how fast you go. All that counts is your heart beat. You want your heart beating at the 70% rate for 30 minutes.

WHY WOG?

Wogging is an aerobic exercise, that is, it creates exertion for both the heart and lungs. Being a combination of walking and jogging it is the best of either. It is better than walking because it burns more calories. It allows you to exercise with prudence. Jogging can be hard on the body. I've seen a lot of joggers develop a number of annoying troubles. Rare is the wogger who experiences the same problems as the jogger.

And because the body is not taxed as much as in jogging, the BHMD exercise is far more likely to become a regular part of your life. A high proportion of people who get into jogging fail to continue because they don't like it. My principle in this matter is, "Train. Don't strain." Therefore, you will like to wog, and you'll want to keep wogging for as long as you live.

Because wogging entails no extraordinary strain, you will look forward to your daily wog with pleasure rather than with dread. Because the exertion is kept within bounds, you'll like to wog not only for weight loss and fitness but also for pure enjoyment. Your delight will increase when in a few weeks you notice the change in your body and attitude. You'll discover a new zest for life. There's no better incentive than that to keep on wogging.

WOGGING FOR HEALTH

If you wish to know why exercise is necessary, I feel like quoting, "Let me count the ways . . ."

But let me begin from the standpoint of weight loss. Wogging alone will not melt away the fat you want to get rid of. Only your Beverly Hills Medical Diet can. Wogging, however, will burn off enough fat to give your figure — especially around the thighs, hips and buttocks — a firm clean contour. While losing weight your body may still retain a certain softness. There may still be some lumps and bumps. Wogging will turn those irregularities into solid substance. Rather than just looking slim, you will actually look muscular.

There is another benefit to wogging that will do your diet a world of good. It may be hard to believe but moderate exercise like wogging actually curbs your appetite. The story would be different if you were to play a hockey or football game, or play basketball. Exertion of this kind is liable to raise a ravenous hunger. But wogging, especially after getting your "wogging legs," is a fantastic relaxer. It even relaxes your desire for food or snacks! Try it and see.

After this exposition I've not yet mentioned the most important reason for exercise. Remember, the BHMD is also a Longevity Plan. At the center of this program is *your heart.*

The amazing BHMD weight loss, the wonderful menus, and your new less stressful mode of living do as much for your heart as a diet possibly can. But without exercise the heart would not yet receive its full due. A vital piece would be missing from your picture of trimness and health without the minumum 30-minute daily wog. From this small investment your heart reaps a dividend that is immeasurable.

Why of all exercises is wogging the best for your heart?

Quite simply because without overstraining itself your heart learns to operate better and with greater efficiency. Under the stimulus of wogging your heart improves its capacity to circulate blood through the body. Driven by the wog it is forced to increase its pumping effort, and in so doing it creates whole new networks of tiny blood vessels.

To some extent these networks can actually replace the blocked arteries that cause heart disease. In conjunction with your diet, wogging can alleviate some of the effects of atherosclerosis. Wogging also does wonders for your lungs because it increases the blood's capacity for carrying oxygen. And as more than one psychiatrist has noted an exercise like wogging is great at relieving depression. The improved circulation of blood to the brain seems to chase the blues away.

Wogging is the activity *par excellence* for your heart because it keeps the blood flowing at a sustained pace from the feet on up throughout your body. After a few weeks of wogging your heart will be able to perform the same tasks with less work. This keeps it from wearing down, and allows you to live young to an old age.

CHAPTER SEVEN:

QUESTIONS MY PATIENTS ASK

Q: *What is the BHMD?*
A: The BHMD is a life-long plan of eating. It is not a fad diet that requires two weeks on and two weeks off. It is not a diet that wreaks havoc on your body's physiology and biochemistry.

The BHMD is a natural diet. It is the way our ancestors ate. It promotes slimness and health, vitality, anti-stress and longevity. It has at its basis the Complex Carbohydrates — vegetables, fruits, grains, peas, beans and lentils, as well as low-fat meats, chicken, turkey and low-fat fish.

Q: *How do simple carbohydrates and Complex Carbohydrates affect stress?*
A: The *simple* or *refined* carbohydrates—also called simple sugars—gave carbohydrates as a whole a bad name in the past. They are for the most part simple sugars, such as common table sugar, syrup, honey and molasses. Ingesting these or foods containing them cause your blood sugar to rise high, thereby signaling the pancreas to increase its production of insulin.

Insulin is needed to lower the blood sugar to normal levels. It does this by causing sugar to enter the cells. Sugar that cannot be utilized for energy is converted to fats. Called triglycerides, these fats cause our bodies and the fat cells to swell up, and as the insulin production by the pancreas is often more than needed, the blood sugar often drops precipitously.

To prevent the severe effects of a very low blood sugar there is a mechanism whereby the adrenal gland secretes adrenalin to liberate sugar from the liver. This is really a *stress reaction* and the sugars are stressors. If the sugar drop is rapid in the blood you may feel weak, hungry, faint or sweaty. If the drop is slow you may feel fatigued or irritable.

The body utilizes sugar for energy but handling the 50-100 calories per minute from our high refined (simple) carbohydrate foods is more than our body was designed to do. The result is both that you don't feel well and carry increased pounds of unwanted fat.

Finally, the refined carbohydrates require digestion and metabolism the same as any other foodstuff. Unfortunately, the vitamins, minerals, enzymes and fiber needed for digestion and elimination have been refined out of the original food. Consequently, these refined substances, in addition to causing the above deleterious actions, actually *rob* the body of its various nutrients which are necessary to metabolize the simple sugars.

The Complex Carbohydrates, on the other hand, are vegetables, fruits, grains, peas, beans, lentils and nuts. These are what we call polysaccharides (*poly* means 'many' and *saccharides* refers to sugars). The Complex Carbohydrate sugars are usually tightly bound together and contain bulk (so you can't eat too much of them). They also contain enzymes, vitamins and minerals which are necessary for their digestion.

The body receives, as a rule, only 2-3 calories per minute. This is easily handled by the body which utilizes them for energy. There is no "robbing" of the body's vitamins, minerals and enzymes to metabolize the C.C. The fiber provides bulk to help satiate the appetite and actually reduces the amount of calories obtained from these unrefined carbohydrates (especially when eaten raw).

The beneficial use of fiber has been well elucidated by others in the reduction of cancer of the colon, hiatal hernia, hemorrhoids, appendicitis and diverticular disease of the colon.

The benefits therefore include a) lowering of excess weight, b) curbing of appetite, c) general wellbeing, and d) no stress reactions because of high and then low blood sugars.

Q: *What is the scientific evidence concerning the effectiveness of the high Complex Carbohydrate and low-protein diet in weight loss?*
A: Literally legion!

The evidence has been around for decades, but it has become more prominent in recent years due to the popularity of hazardous diets such as those promoted by Scarsdale and Atkins.

I have no room to cite all the studies extolling the diet similar to the BHMD. Suffice it to quote from a very recent experiment reported by Jane Brody in the *New York Times* this year. In the experiment conducted at the University of Virginia two groups of adult animals were fed diets with approximately the same number of calories. However, the food consumed by one group contained 25 percent of its calories in protein; the other group ate food containing only 5 percent of its calories in protein.

"At the end of the experiment," noted the article, "the animals that ate the high-protein had on the average nearly 23.9 percent of their body-weight accounted for by fat. But the low-protein group had only 15.6 percent of its weight as fat."

The high-protein group weighed 22 percent *more* than the low-protein group.

"If the findings in rats have any bearings on human obesity," concluded Jane Brody, "they suggest that the best way to lose weight is to follow a diet low in fat and protein and very high in complex carbohydrates, such as grains, vegetables and fruits."

Q: *What about fat? Will I get enough fat in the BHMD?*
A: Fat is ubiquitous. It is found in all foods we eat. Would you believe romaine lettuce has fat? Likewise asparagus and all vegetables. Fruits, too, have fats. So do cereals. There's no way to avoid fats. You'll get enough fat in the BHMD and you won't get too much.

Q: *How severe are the dangers of the fats we get in our average ordinary American diet?*
A: My studies have shown that we get 40-50 percent of our total calories from fat. Often teenaged girls may get as high as 55 percent of total calories as fat.

Fat adds unwanted pounds to our bodies. Eating lots of fat causes a thin film of fat to adhere to the red blood cells (the cells that carry oxygen to our tissues). This causes the red blood cell to take on less oxygen than it is able to. It is one of the reasons you may see people lethargic or falling asleep after a heavy meal.

I have seen increased fats in the blood minutes after a meal of salad with oil and vinegar was eaten. Fats, animal and vegetable, together with cholesterol, which is found in foods of animal origin, have been incriminated in coronary artery disease, arteriosclerosis and a myriad of other illnesses.

Q: *Don't we need extra protein supplements in our diets in order to feel good?*
A: There is absolutely no benefit in excess protein, and the BHMD provides all the protein you require.

Protein is not stored in the body like other substances. Whatever the body cannot use to make tissues is broken down and stored as fat and cannot be changed back to protein.

Furthermore, the huge excesses of protein in our diets causes calcium (and other minerals) to be lost in the urine. Calcium losses, in time, help to demineralize the bones may account for a large number of spontaneous bone fractures each year.

Q: *But I've always been told that a high-protein diet is necessary for strength and endurance.*

A: Just the opposite is true. It is a myth that you need a large amount of protein, especially animal protein, for strength and endurance.

Studies performed by many exercise physiologists show that the high Complex Carbohydrate diet is far superior to the high-protein diet when strength, endurance and wellbeing are evaluated.

As a matter of fact, studies have shown that endurance tends to decrease as protein intake increases. In one of those studies medical students were put on a treadmill and exercised to exhaustion after they had been on a high-protein diet. The same routine, conducted after a high-Complex Carbohydrate diet like the BHMD indicated that endurance was very much increased.

The most common complaint that I, as a physician, hear is, "Doc, I'm tired." Almost invariably upon a change from the high-protein/high-fat diet to the BHMD, the patient experiences a newfound energy and zest.

Q: *May the BHMD help prevent hearing loss?*

A: Hearing loss is very prevalent in our society, but the most important reason I believe is due to nutrition: our high-fat diet. The ears are supplied with nourishment by rather small arteries which don't have much communication with other arteries. Because of fat, these arteries clog up and hearing loss is often the result. Some lessening of hearing defects may theoretically take place when the high-fat diet has been changed to the low-fat BHMD.

The great composer Ludwig Von Beethoven (1770-1827) lost much of his hearing by age 30 and eventually became deaf. At the autopsy, the arteries of the ears were found to be clogged with fat particles and the auditory nerves had consequently degenerated.

Q: *Will I need my high blood pressure medicine when I am on the BHMD?*
A: This can only be determined by your physician. Do not stop your medication unless advised to do so by your physician.

High blood pressure often leads to strokes, heart failure, kidney failure and arteriosclerosis. About one in every two adults has or will have high blood pressure.

In utilizing the BHMD I have found most patients with high blood pressure need little or no medication.

Q: *Is there really any good evidence that the low-fat, low-salt, high-Complex Carbohydrate BHMD will help lower the heart attack rate?*
A: Yes. I have seen startling changes in the reversal of this disease in the past 10 years, but some of the best evidence was contained in a 5-year study conducted in Finland. This study sought to reduce the incidence of heart attack and stroke involving 180,000 people in Eastern Finland, an area with the highest heart attack rate in the world due to the dietary prevalence of high cholesterol, as well as such factors as high blood pressure and cigarette smoking.

After a massive program to change the dietary and smoking habits was begun in 1972, a 30-40 percent decrease in strokes occured. A marked decrease in high blood pressure became evident in 17,000 registered hypertensives. The annual incidence rates of heart attacks decreased by more than 15%. The people in the study had brought about these results by increasing the use of low-fat milk. They had cut down on butter and sausages and raised the consumption of vegetables.

It does pay to follow the precepts of the BHMD!

Q: *Can the BHMD cause plugged up arteries to become unplugged.*
A: Evidence is coming in showing reversibility of arteries narrowed by fat. Angiographic studies indicate regression of narrowed arteries on the BHMD-type diet. Individual reversibility has been found in animals such as pigs, monkeys and pigeons, due to an arteriosclerotic reversal diet similar to the BHMD.

Q: *Will losing weight lessen the various risk factors for coronary disease that I do have?*
A: Absolutely. I have seen it in innumerable patients who lost weight. By losing fat their risk factors improved due to the lowering in the body of the bad cholesterols, blood sugar and uric acid.

Q: *What about exercise for old people? Is it advisable?*
A: Not only is it advisable, it is mandatory if you want to live a long, healthy, happy life. My twenty-year study of patients who have lived up till ages 90-100

has taught me that although many factors enter into longevity, frequent exercise on a regular basis is one of the most important.

Q: *What about long life. Does the BHMD play a part in longevity?*
A: Without doubt.

Let me tell you about a patient that I met when he was 95 years old.

A careful examination failed to reveal any body abnormalities. His blood pressure was an excellent 110/ 80. His serum cholesterol was a low 150, and the HDL (the good cholesterol) was at a proper level of 65 — protective against coronary artery disease. His triglycerides (the blood fats) were a good low 50 mg %.

He told me that he never liked fatty foods such as butter, and when margarine became fashionable he didn't like that either. He got the bulk of his calories from vegetables, fruits, grains, peas, beans and lentils. He ingested low fat fish, chicken or turkey without the skins. He never used much in the way of cakes or pies and ate only whole wheat bread. He never used stimulants or junk foods.

Although he didn't have to do hard work, he knew that when farm animals didn't work they didn't last too long, so he made time each day for walking.

Q: *Does dietary cholesterol really have anything to do with the blood cholesterol?*
A: Absolutely.

The dietary cholesterol is related to the serum cholesterol. Dr. Castelli of the famous Framingham study tells us that for every 100 mg of cholesterol intake the serum cholesterol will be elevated by 5 mg %. One egg yolk, according to him, is worth 12½ mg %.

I don't put all my patients on a restricted cholesterol diet, for some people seem to have a built-in protective device that prevents a rise in cholesterol. Get your cholesterol checked. If it is around 150 mg %, you can feel pretty good. I have not heard of any case of coronary artery disease with a cholesterol in that range.

Q: *Does diet affect your sexual being? Can the BHMD help your sexuality?*
A: The connection between good health and good sex has been well established. The strain of carrying excess weight as seen in obese persons is not only a physical but also an emotional deterrant to good sexual relations.

Obesity itself is a major stressor. My observations on people who have followed the BHMD for reducing is that sexuality as well as energy are enhanced. Sexuality, after all, is part of a healthy life. When you're feeling good — and feeling good about yourself — your sexual drive is enhanced.

51

Q: *Can the BHMD affect menstruation?*

A: I have seen case after case of younger women who had abnormal menses often associated with pain and weight gain. Quite a few of these women told me that "for 1-2 weeks out of the month I'm not a functioning woman." After going on the BHMD they not only gained a new figure, but in addition the abnormal menses they had experienced were normalized.

By the way, the high-fat diet consumed in this country has been found to result in hormonal changes, such as earlier onset of menses.

Q: *I have heard that our average diet promotes breast cancer in women. Is that true?*

A: Correct.

An increased incidence of cancer of the breast in American-born daughters of Japanese women who move to the U.S. has been documented. High-fat diets promote breast cancer in the incidence of spontaneous and chemically-induced breast cancer in rats. It is believed that a regular high-fat intake promotes breast cancer by raising the level of the pituitary hormone, prolactin.

Q: *What are vitamins?*

A: Vitamins are really accessory food factors (organic compunds found in plants and animals). Necessary for our growth, reproduction and good health, they are required in small quantities in order to avoid a vitamin deficiency.

Vitamins are the "spark plugs of life" and, as such, they function in body metabolism as an essential part of the enzyme systems of the body.

Q: *Where do we get our vitamins?*

A: All vitamins are present in the foods we eat. However, many can be destroyed in the packing, storing, preparing and cooking process.

Q: *Does the BHMD provide adequate vitamins and minerals?*

A: The BHMD does provide adequate vitamins and minerals but because of excess demands made upon us by external factors we need additional vitamins to lift us to the optimal state of health.

Q: *Are minerals essential for good health?*

A: There are essential minerals necessary for growth and development of our bodies. There are toxic minerals also. These may poison the body. Lead and mercury are poisonous minerals and they interfere with enzyme systems of the body. Other poisonous minerals include cadmium, aluminum and arsenic.

The essential minerals such as calcium, magnesium, phosphorous, sodium and potassium are found in the body in large amounts. Ninety-nine percent of all the calcium in the body is found in the bones and teeth.

Other necessary minerals such as iron, copper, manganese, zinc, chromium and selenium are found in the body in small amounts.

Q: *Are diuretics safe for weight loss?*
A: Doctors prescribe diuretics for high blood pressure and/or swelling of the body. However, I have found that even a small amount of diuretics may "wash out" many of the essential minerals.

Although minerals are not destroyed by heat (like some vitamins) they may be lost in the cooking process and are usually poorly absorbed from the digestive tract. For example, only 10% of ingested iron and only 4-8% of ingested chromium is absorbed.

Q: *How much in the way of vitamins and minerals do I need above the diet I consume?*
A: If you are consuming a diet which is high in sugar and refined flour you are losing lots of vitamins. Foods eaten whole contain their own vitamins and minerals necessary for the digestive process. However, refined products (cakes, pies, candy, and other processed foods) "rob" the body of vitamins and some minerals in order that the digestive process take place.

Q: *What vitamins and minerals should I take?*
A: I can't recommend vitamins and minerals for you individually. Everyone's needs are different. You should check with your physician. However, I do believe that *most* people can benefit with the basic vitamins and minerals.

Q: *What will the BHMD do for night cravings?*
A: If you are a 'midnight muncher' you are not alone. Many overweight people consume the bulk of their calories after six o'clock in the evening. Some are unable to sleep without a stomach full of food. Still others awaken in the night and remain insomniac until they have satisfied their night craving for food, usually carbohydrates.

The BHMD emphasis on Complex Carbohydrates ensures a more stable blood-sugar count. Since Complex Carbohydrates are absorbed into the bloodstream evenly and smoothly, the sugar level is not bouncing up and down — the reason for hunger cravings. If you keep to the BHMD method of eating-all-the-time on permissible foods you won't get the "munchies" and you won't gain weight.

Q: *How or why is it that I satisfy my appetite so easily on the BHMD?*
A: The reason there is quick satiation of appetite is that the Complex Carbo-hydrates–the mainstay of the BHMD–provide the bulk for quickly filling up the stomach. One way you can help to "fill up quickly" is to take your time eating. Chew thoroughly and slowly. Give your stomach a chance to signal to your brain that it is full.

Q: *What do I do about hunger pangs on the BHMD?*
A: Eat all day long *and* eat in-between meals and when hungry from the special list of the raw Complex Carbohydrates. Carry them with you all day.

Q: *How do I explain to people that I'm trying to lose weight?*
A: Tell them right up front, "I'm on the BHMD for my weight, my health, because I want to look and feel good, and because it's the safest and most effective way to lose weight and to eat for the rest of my life. Don't hinder me; help me."

Q: *Why do I feel dizzy and 'draggy' on high-protein diets?*
A: Those fad diets invariably cause bad symptoms such as weakness, fatigue, dizziness, etc. because such diets derange the metabolism of the body.

The usual mechanism — especialy in the high-protein diet — is the tremendous loss of minerals such as potassium (so important in heart and muscle metabolism), as well as loss of other vital nutrients including calcium, magnesium, zinc, chromium, *and* vitamin loss.

There is also the ketosis which is so dangerous that when we doctors see patients in ketosis with diabetes mellitus, lactic acidosis or other disorders we treat it in a hospital as a medical emergency.

In addition, there is a large water loss which causes a 'hemo-concentration' – an actual thickening of the blood due to a loss of fluid from the blood itself. This and other factors in fad diets cause many metabolic problems for the dieter. Some of these problems are downright dangerous to the dieter.

Q: *How does the BHMD differ from the high-protein diets in relation to heart disease?*

A: The BHMD is *safe;* the high-protein diets are *dangerous.* The other diets don't pay any attention to the heart. They ignore the fact that the high-protein/ low-carbohydrate diet is actually a high-fat diet. It has been shown that these diets raise the cholesterol and fats, producing conditions that invariably lead to narrowing of arteries in the heart, as well as in the brain, kidney, and other parts of the body.

The BHMD is also a high-fiber diet and the high-protein diet is not a high-fiber diet. Fiber is necessary to help reduce the high fats and cholesterol and prevent them from clogging up the arteries.

Our immune system's effectiveness is reduced by the stress of the high-protein/high-fat diet and many now believe this leads to more illnesses of a serious nature. The BHMD actually helps to stimulate the immune system, thus improving our chances of leading a long and healthy life.

Q: *Why do people on the high-protein diet feel so thirsty?*
A: There is a great deal of water required to metabolize protein — some seven times as much water as is needed to metabolize carbohydrate. The weight loss — especially initially — is largely water. This in turn helps cause tissue dehydration, producing wrinkles, aging and all sorts of potentially serious problems.

Q: *Is it true that some people have actually died on the high-protein diet?*
A: The deaths attributed to high-protein diets that were reported in the prestigious *New England Journal of Medicine* were due to the serious *cardiac arrhythmias* – irregularities of the heart. These were caused by losses of potassium, magnesium, other minerals and by the accumulation of metabolic wastes of the proteins.

Q: *How does the fiber in the BHMD help to lose weight?*
A: Fiber in the foods we eat helps us to feel full much quicker than when we eat refined foods. Therefore we don't tend to eat as much. Think of how much candy or cake one may eat as compared to say baked potatoes or steamed broccoli?

Additionally, when you eat high-fiber foods you really don't get all the calories in the food. That's because frequently the food — especially raw foods — are not completely broken down and therefore not completely metabolized. Therefore less weight is gained and more weight is lost for equal weights of high-fiber food as compared to refined foods.

Because the time taken for food to pass through the intestinal tract is decreased with high-fiber foods the absorption of calories is decreased and, of course, more weight is lost.

High-fiber foods especially vegetables are mostly water and undigestible fiber. The potato has about 77% of its weight in water. Many vegetables range from the 70's to the 90's% in water. Water has no calories!

Q: *Are there any problems associated with a high-fiber diet?*
A: There may be some gas for 2-4 weeks.

55

Q: *Can exercise cause a heart attack?*

A: A heart attack is caused by the gradual narrowing, culminating in the closure of a coronary artery. If a person has coronary artery disease, exercise of the type that is strenuous may throw an extra burden on the already narrowed coronary artery and possibly precipitate a heart attack.

However, one of the best ways to avoid a heart attack, in addition to the BHMD, is to take a daily walk, and if there is no contraindication, wogging. Seek your doctor's advice before starting the exercise program.

Q: *What about high blood pressure? Can the BHMD lower high blood pressure?*

A: My experience with patients over a long period of time has clearly shown that using the BHMD to lower weight will result in the lowering of blood pressure. As a result, in many cases the need for high blood pressure medications will *not* be required.

Q: *Will the Beverly Hills Diet help the person with diabetes mellitus?*

A: It is well known that an overweight adult with diabetes mellitus usually has more insulin in the body than is needed — perhaps 2-3 times as much as normal.

However, because of the overlarge fat cells and the large amount of blood fats the cells are not sensitive to insulin. Therefore, insulin is hardly effective in lowering blood sugar. It has been shown that as you lower the weight (and thereby the fat) the diabetics become more sensitive to their own insulin.

Q: *Can the BHMD do anything about constipation?*

A: One of the common complaints of people on the "other" diets is that they suffer from constipation. However, I have never yet heard this complaint from my patients who follow the BHMD, which is a diet rich in Complex Carbohydrates. Such a diet is also rich in the grains and fiber that provide roughage. Constipation will not occur on any diet in which these two elements play a prominent role.

Q: *I suffer from hemorrhoids. Will they disappear on the BHMD?*

A: Hemorrhoids are simply damaged veins situated about the anus. They are yet another toll we pay for our addiction to highly refined foods without sufficient bulk. The painfulness of the hemorrhoids is caused by the hardened fecal matter pressing on the veins.

The Complex Carbohydrate diet with its high-roughage content alters the solid, dry consistency of the stool. This means less strain in passing it and a subsequent lessening of pressure on the hemorrhoidal veins. The BHMD cannot "repair" those veins, but it can ease the pressure on them and also keep new hemorrhoids from forming.

Q: *Can the BHMD forestall cancer of the colon?*
A: Cancer of the colon, it is now argued, is caused by fecal matter that is retained inordinately long in the large intestine. There a chemical process takes place resulting in the formation of cancer-producing compounds. The high-fiber contents of the BHMD stimulate a more rapid passage of the fecal matter, thus preventing the build-up of carcinogenic compounds and the resultant risk of cancer of the colon.

CHAPTER EIGHT:

CHANGE YOUR SELF-IMAGE ON THE BHMD

PICTURE YOURSELF SLIM

Your goals should be first those of health and vitality. Everything else is secondary to good health, both physically and emotionally. Being slim is often a reflection of good health. The BHMD helps you take the steps that are needed to get you under way toward all these objectives.

If you are overweight see yourself slim, trim and vital. Keep that picture in your mind. Think upon it throughout the day. It can do wonders.

In addition to visualizing yourself slim several times or more a day, what else can you do to keep your object in sight? You may want to use several artificial reinforcements. A 3″ x 5″ card on which you've written your goal can serve as a positive reminder when you find your will slackening.

Tape the card by your bed, in your bathroom mirror, at the dining table, on the dashboard of your automobile, on the desk where you work, inside the refrigerator. In other words, keep that goal always in sight. It keeps you charged up and increases your enthusiasm to stick to your diet.

The history of Cheryl Tiegs, the famous cover girl model is a case in point. She once weighed a very unmodellike 150 pounds. Today she is the picture of glamorous beauty. How did she lose weight? "You must put yourself in the right state of mind," she says, "and be determined to make yourself the best you can be."

Cheryl Tiegs stays slim today because she works at it. "I have to be conscious of what I eat and how much." Cheryl lost weight and stays slim because she put herself in the right frame of mind and adopted a successful concept of herself. Likewise, part of what I do is to help people motivate themselves. I try to get them to take over responsibility for their weight loss and health.

I don't mean that they should go out and buy a scalpel and do their own appendectomy. I'm merely suggesting that they should start by learning about their own body. I want them to know what it takes to get their body to work right so they can have optimal health.

By following the rules, by reducing or eliminating the destructive health habits, they improve their Self-Image.

INCREASE THE POSSIBLE

What is this Self-Image? The self-image is what you really think of yourself. If you are overweight and wish to reduce, the self-image of a fat person may foil your efforts to get slim. It is therefore important to shed your old self-image along with your unwanted pounds.

On the BHMD, as your physical appearance changes from an overweight to a slim person, it is important to change your self-image likewise. If you don't have a good self-image you will have a more difficult time. Most likely you will not accomplish that which you deserve and are capable of.

A poor self-image reduces your capability. It reduces what is possible for you. It increases the area of the impossible in your life. It makes you resigned to an overweight self-image. The BHMD keeps you permanently slim, and that's how it permanently alters the way you perceive yourself.

A great number of my patients have worked marvels in their personality by following the BHMD. Simply by losing weight and feeling less stressful, they began to blossom as persons. They made new friends, experienced better relationships and found better jobs. How the BHMD can change your self-image positively may be shown by one case history.

Mrs. S.H., a 46-year-old woman, 5'5", 180 lbs. Suffers from high blood pressure and mild diabetes mellitus. Extremely unhappy with herself.

Despite medications her blood pressure, diabetes and weight remained problems. Has gone from one diet to another with no appreciable results.

When asked how she perceived herself, she finally answered that she thought very little of herself. Who do you think of first? "My children." Second? "My husband." Third? "My mother." Fourth? "My sisters."

I explained about the Self-Image to her and how my diet would help her look at herself more positively. By thinking well of herself, I pointed out, she would actually do a service to her husband, mother and sisters. She would be able to relate to them better because by having her weight under control she would become more agreeable in every respect.

She followed the diet and soon the impossible became possible. She lost weight easily on the BHMD. The blood pressure and diabetes mellitus normalized and she no longer required medications.

SELF-IMAGE AND STRESS

The ideas of which we are speaking can also be used to help lessen the severity or abolish physical symptoms of diseases which are caused by stress.

Stress, as we perceive it, is integrated in a part of the brain called the hypothalamus and from there the adrenal gland is stimulated to make adrenalin (Epinephrine) which raises blood pressure, speeds up the heart rate and increases the rate of breathing. It also tightens skeletal muscles, especially those of the head, neck, shoulders and back. It increases our white cells, red cells and platelets and increases the ability of our blood to clot, setting off the terrible feelings of anxiety.

The hypothalamus also stimulates the pituitary gland (the "Master Gland"), which in turn stimulates the Adrenal Gland to produce cortisone-like substances.

With stress after stress after stress, our immune system is depressed by the cortisone and we lose much of our body's defense against bacteria, viruses and perhaps even against cancer. Because of continued stress we develop all kinds of symptoms of aches, pains, fatigue, sexual dysfunction, overeating, increased anxiety, depression and many other symptoms – our body's way of trying to tell us to change our mode of living.

With the body so upset from the Stress Reaction, it is no wonder that we get sick, or are unable to stick to a diet. But the BHMD means nutrition that reduces stress while you lose weight. At the same time it improves your self-image, because the proof of your determination becomes immediately evident. Just look at the story of one of my patients who through the BHMD not only lost weight but also managed to stem several serious illnesses.

BT, a 25-year-old man with a history of severe colitis which was controlled. Becoming frustrated and dissatisfied with his work and mode of living, he gained weight. Frustrated at every turn, he developed severe abdominal pain and diarrhea.

Decided to follow the BHMD and agreed to work on setting goals toward getting a new and better job in Public Relations. As soon as he dropped five pounds after six days of dieting, he became a changed man. His success on the diet no longer led him to see himself as weak and ineffectual. He lost seventeen pounds in one month. And as he worked toward this goal he also lost the painful symptoms.

This brings me up to the last point which has to do with getting a new habit. It is called the winning habit. Losing weight can become a winning habit.

With the principles of the BHMD as a lifelong objective, you acquire a habit that spreads its ripples of success throughout all areas of your life. You will gain a new self-image which in turn helps keep you from ever letting yourself go and become overweight again.

CHAPTER NINE:

DINING OUT WITH THE BHMD

AVOID TRAGEDY

The dieter's path, as you well know, is riddled with pitfalls. Temptations to break the rules are present everywhere. Yet, you are stout of heart. Your will is iron. You persist on the BHMD, and soon, as your excess fat melts off and as your new eating habits take over, dieting has become a breeze.

Then comes the tragedy.

You are invited out, either to a restaurant or a party, and there your resolve collapses. You nibble and eat all those forbidden foods while you console yourself, "It's just this once." As you reach for another fattening hors d'oeuvre, you tell yourself that the next day you will eat less: instead of an hour of wogging, you will wog two.

Your intentions may be the best. Unfortunately, more likely than not, your diet is in ruin.

The problem of dining out and parties is one every dieter who follows the BHMD has to tackle head on. It's best to prepare and gird yourself beforehand against the dangers of free-wheeling buffets and restaurant menus. There are many ways in which you can do this. Let's begin with a party – *your party*.

THE BHMD COCKTAIL PARTY

The party you are throwing at your home might serve as an initiation both for you and your friends in the BHMD way-of-eating. It will help you in accustoming yourself to sticking to the diet in the most tempting situations. It is also a way of letting your guests know that it is possible to have a merry get-together that is nutritionally sound and physically slimming. You may even be surprised at the "ripple effect" it is likely to cause among your friends. Certainly, your small festivity may be far from the last "BHMD Cocktail Party" you're attending.

To begin, place on your buffet table a large assortment of colorfully arranged raw carrot sticks, slightly steamed broccoli, raw cauliflower, celery sticks, jicama (very popular in California), cooked artichokes, cooked asparagus, hearts of palm, etc. The colorful display is sure to delight your guests.

When it comes to the "cocktails" allow your inventiveness to take over. Serve sparkling mineral water in wine or champagne glasses. You may want to add a dash of cranberry concentrate or apple juice concentrate (both no sugar added). Or pass around a tray of Virgin Mary's, using tomato juice from the refrigerator spiced up with fresh vegetables.

Once you've gotten into the habit of carrying your diet through thick and thin (to coin a phrase!), you'll find the going easier in situations that are not entirely under your personal control. You want to maintain your newly won figure. You do not want to swerve from the straight road of nutritional health. Paramount in your mind is the desire to stick to the BHMD. All these resolutions will make it easier when you are invited outside your home to be firm in passing up tidbits and dishes that go against the diet.

In this connection it is not at all unreasonable to inform your host or hostess in advance of your food limitations. After all, many people suffer from ailments which curb the use of salt, sugar, fats, etc. There is no need to be embarrassed to confide to those who have requested your company that you must abide by similar restraints.

Inform them that you must eat your vegetables plain, not floating in butter or margarine, and that plain broiled fish or chicken would suit you to perfection. It is very likely that your wishes not only will be respected, but that you make new converts to the healthy weight-loss fare of the BHMD.

63

IN RESTAURANTS

Many of my patients eat two or more meals out in restaurants daily. Yet, they experience no conflict with the BHMD way-of-eating. They stay healthy, fit and trim. How do they do it?

Many of my patients are, of course, seasoned veterans of the BHMD. They have learned to sail with skill between the shoals of fats and sugars. Because of their sound snacking habits they are never overtaken by hunger cravings. They munch on some permissible foods all day, and by virtue of the little "baggies" they carry they are never ravenous when they reach the restaurant. They spend a lot of time at the salad bar. They are not shy to ask the waiter to have their food prepared according to the BHMD. They search the menu carefully, and rather than wolfing down lots of white bread and butter they spend the waiting time in conversation and sipping water.

We are fortunate today that many restaurants are tuned to the needs of their patrons. A salad bar used to be a rarity; now it is rare *not* to see one. In Beverly Hills, where diet-consciousness is widespread, my patients have no difficulty in following the BHMD while eating out due to the many fine restaurants and the wide varieties of foods. But I believe that you can choose carefully and maintain the BHMD habit no matter where you live.

The salad should always be an important part of your restaurant dinner – a safe way to fill you up without packing your body with calories. However, beware of such dressings as roquefort cheese, thousand island, or oil and vinegar: they are terribly high in fat. Instead, ask the waiter to bring some crushed garlic and mix it with the vinegar. Or order a glass of orange juice, or a lemon.

You may also want to carry your own salad dressing in a plastic container – That is, Win -Vin Dressing or one of the many other delicious low-cal salad dressings described in this book.

Though the salad bar is a great help to your BHMD habit, it should still be approached with caution. Pickled beets, canned kidney beans and canned garbanzo beans, being loaded with hidden salts and sugars, are a definite no-no. Also beware of fatty, undesirable substances such as bacon bits, olives and pickles. Invariably I see people in restaurants load their plates at the salad bar with the best foods, only to ruin it with high-fat dressings, bacon bits and garbanzo beans.

For better nutrition you're best off picking out the dark leafy lettuce or spinach rather than iceberg lettuce. The dark green lettuce and spinach have lots of nutrients, while there are next to none in the iceberg lettuce.

When it comes to the main dish, don't order anything fried. Instruct the waiter not to use butter or margarine on your foods. Stick to broiled, steamed or poached fish and chicken seasoned, if you wish, with fresh lemon, vinegar and/or pepper.

Eat only baked potatoes and garnish them with lemon, pepper and chives. Load up on vegetables as much as you like, but be careful: many restaurants feel compelled to smother vegetables in butter.

When eating breakfast out, you can't go wrong ordering oatmeal *without* butter. A little bit of skim milk, and if you're not trying to lose weight, some fresh fruit added to the oatmeal makes an excellent start for the day. An orange or freshly squeezed orange juice with the pulp still in it is fine.

Many of the dangers of eating out can be avoided at a "health food" or vegetarian restaurant. But it is wise to be cautious. A few of these establishments tend to serve large amounts of cheese and oils. Regular cheeses are 65-70% of their calories in fat, as contrasted with cheese made from skim-milk – very low in fat.

Tell the waiter to omit cheese and oil from your foods. If you order a fruit salad, make sure the fruit is fresh. If it comes from a can its nutritional value is practically zero and also high in sugar and syrup.

Finally, you may be spared all the bother of picking and choosing by calling ahead and letting the restauranteur know of your special needs. The better restaurants will be glad to accommodate you. You may want to do the same for banquets, weddings and other special occasions. I have found that by calling ahead in these cases I not only get the foods I want but most of the time my dish is superior to the usual fatty chicken or steak and potatoes normally served at such events.

GO ETHNIC

Yes, ethnic restaurants, believe it or not, usually offer menu choices closest to the BHMD. Unlike the high-fat, high-protein Western diet of steak, buttered breads, and gravies, most ethnic specialties are high in the elements that make up the BHMD. Even many Mexican and Italian dishes that are noted for their high calorie content can be modified when eaten out. For instance:

Mexican – Stay away from tacos and enchiladas. Order a tostada loaded with vegetables. If there's too much beans or meat mixture, clear off the excess and leave just enough to add flavor to the salad on top.

As an appetizer order some plain steamed corn tortillas and eat these with chile sauce. Each tortilla is packed with valuable fiber and has only 50 calories. Avoid the chips that restaurants serve as fillers: they're usually packed with hidden calories and fats.

Japanese – Many Japanese restaurants serve dishes with lots of vegetables and little animal protein. Avoid tempura and order sukiyaki-style dishes or chicken teriyaki. As in all restaurants, remove skins and fats from all meats. Many Japanese restaurants feature raw fish and steamed fish, both of which are extremely low in calories.

Italian – Your best bet in an Italian restaurant is broiled fish "Italian style" and an order of plain pasta and salad. Pour a little vinegar or lemon on the salad. If you can't resist the sauce for the pasta, have it brought on the side and only use one or two tablespoons.

Chinese Restaurants – Chinese restaurants are good because they will cook your food to order. Ask the chef to prepare chicken and vegetables without the MSG, sugar, salt and oil. Use a little soy sauce instead of oily sauces to give food more flavor.

Seafood – Go light on the high-cholesterol shellfish. Butter and tartar sauces are out, as is frying. Have seafood broiled, baked or poached. If it comes with a rich cream sauce, scrape off the sauce and season with pepper and lemon. (See the *Fish Hint* p. 80).

DIET AND TRAVEL

It is one of the principles of the BHMD to keep your stomach filled, so you won't be tempted to munch on taboo foods. When traveling prepare yourself with a thermos, baggies and sealed-plastic containers stocked with permissible items.

Good dishes for travel include bean salads, cole slaw, low-fat cottage cheese, salad, chicken salad, dips, vegetables, tuna sandwiches. The idea is not to starve yourself. Therefore, eat every few hours. Go for an apple or a banana if you're desperate, but eat something.

When traveling by plane, boat, or if you have been invited to a picnic, it's advisable to ask what they serve. Regulate yourself accordingly. Don't leave the house hungry and bring what you deem consistent with the BHMD to satisfy your stomach.

GUIDE TO EATING OUT

These are some suggestions for following the BHMD in restaurants. Remember to be selective wherever you are – no refined grains or sugars, no fats, little or no salt.

1. Don't eat the bread or rolls while waiting.
2. Drink water – and nothing else. (Natural mineral water, such as Perrier water, with lemon or lime, or Linden tea is acceptable.)
3. Don't order *anything* fried. Order foods such as:
   - *steamed* vegetables or fish
   - *poached* fish
   - *baked* potatoes, vegetables or fish
   - *broiled* fish
4. *Don't be shy!* Ask to have your food prepared in accordance with the BHMD. If the restaurant refuses, go elsewhere.
5. Use only vinegar, lemon juice, tomato juice or fruit juice as dressing on tossed salad.
6. If your salad is unappealing, or nothing but lettuce, order sliced tomatoes, ½ a cantaloupe, ½ a grapefruit, or other raw fruits or vegetables.
7. When at a salad bar pick mostly *raw* vegetables. Pickled beets, canned kidney or garbanzo beans all contain sugar! Beware of salad ingredients such as bacon bits, olives, pickles, etc.
8. Don't order dessert (or eat anyone else's). Have fresh fruit instead.
9. Ask the waiter if the fruit in the fruit bowl is fresh or canned, or if the vegetables are cooked in butter, or if there is oil or sugar in the salad dressing, etc.
10. Don't eat everything on your plate just because you paid for it. When you have had enough to eat, *stop eating!*
11. Social dining is fun, but you may not be able to control the restaurant selection. Eat something healthy at home before you go out – then eat lightly at the restaurant.

CHAPTER TEN:

ON HOLIDAY WITH THE BHMD

PARTY DIETS

Holidays always present a threat to your waistline. The temptation to overeat while eating out is never so great as during the Christmas holidays. Cocktail parties, dinner parties, and family reunions make this the most critical time of the year for the maintenance of your diet.

Following are some ways to *at least* maintain your weight – and perhaps, with enough will power, even shed a few pounds.

1. Go on the BHMD Plunge as the holiday season approaches. Take off several excess pounds before the holidays arrive, so a few "excesses" will be permissible.

2. *Eat before you eat* and follow the general rules of BHMD: Eat all day from the permissible foods and keep the edge off your hunger.

3. Drink plenty of club soda or water once you arrive at the party.

4. Think of the consequences of overindulgence when you approach that holiday buffet. Load your plate with raw vegetables. Before you reach for that rich canape or fattening dip think of how you'll look with a few more pounds around your middle.

5. Nobody wants to talk diet at holidays so when an overzealous host is

insistent, simply compliment him on the wonderful offerings and
firmly say, "No, thank you."

6. If you are the host give all the leftovers to the guests as they leave.
7. Carry a baggie filled with BHMD goodies and munch in between
   parties.

HOLIDAYS & STRESS

If you stick to the BHMD-prescribed foods during the holidays you'll have a
powerful weapon against the common holiday symptoms of anxiety, stress and
depression. The Complex Carbohydrates as described in the BHMD represent
a form of nutrition with a minimum of stressful components.

A common way of dealing with holiday overindulgence is the crash diet. This
means simply that you're piling up more stress, apart from endangering your
health. "Crash diets will not only throw the body metabolism out of kilter,"
warns Dr. Maria Simonson, "it also ages you faster." A director of the Johns
Hopkins Hospital health and weight program, Dr. Simonson notes: "The skin
may get dry, the lines will show sooner because the body is going through a
major dietary imbalance."

The fact that certain foods help to alleviate common anxieties has also been
observed by Dr. Arnold Andersen, assistant professor of psychiatry at Johns
Hopkins. He has remarked, for instance, how turkey and milk, "have a higher
level of tryptophan which, through increasing serotonin in the brain, has a mild
anti-depressive effect."

This is precisely why it's so important that you stick to the BHMD while on
holiday. The Complex Carbohydrates are your safeguard against overeating
due to stress and anxiety.

CHAPTER ELEVEN:

THE BHMD KITCHEN

WHERE THE STORY BEGINS

The heart of the BHMD is your kitchen. The wonderful transformation that takes place in your physical appearance has its workshop in the place where you prepare your meals.

While you follow the BHMD your kitchen is no longer a place where you slave over a hot oven, dodging the spatters of oil and grease. Oil, grease and fats are taboo in your new way of eating. Instead, the BHMD transforms your kitchen into an adventure. The preparation of each meal becomes a thrilling voyage in a new kind of gastronomy, one that reduces your weight as it takes away stress. In a way, the kitchen becomes your classroom, with the BHMD as your instructor and yourself as the apt chef.

In the kitchen you will learn to cook meals so delicious that dieting soon turns into a greater pleasure than you ever experienced in your days of fattening sauces and heavy meats. The meals you'll be cooking are not only satisfying and appetizing but, more importantly, they are wholesome and slimming. They'll give you the good feeling that comes when you know you are providing yourself and your family with superior nutrition.

The recipes, by virtue of being creative and varied, will teach you techniques hitherto reserved for the grand cooks and professional nutritionists. They are techniques you will be able to utilize in all phases of cookery. What you learn from one recipe about using the oven, for instance, or about the preparation of certain vegetables and grains as scrumptious extenders, can be appplied to many other areas. With this knowledge of new techniques under your steadily crimping belt, you will be able to experiment with dishes of your own creative ingenuity.

"I first believed that cooking a diet as you recommend would be a bore," remarked one housewife to me, "but would you believe that I've become an absolute whizz around the kitchen?" This woman had lost 14 pounds in a little over two weeks by sticking to BHMD-inspired dishes high in Complex Carbohydrates, moderate-to-low in protein, and very low in fat. By reducing her refined sugar intake she had eliminated her low blood sugar problems, and she felt much less stress. And on top of that, she had become an expert cook!

Here are some important pointers for your BHMD kitchen:

Storage

Stock your refrigerator with plenty of cooked beans, rice, and baked potatoes. While making excellent side dishes for many entrees, these high-Complex Carbohydrate foods have an even better use for soups, instant oven fries, dips, and stuffings. A tablespoon of tasty cooked pinto beans or delicious black beans can add tremendous texture and flavor to soups and stews.

Prepare large bags of carrot sticks and celery sticks for snacks, outings, guests and appetizers. By readying a large bag for later use you remove the excuse that it's too difficult or time-consuming.

Keep your spice rack well stocked with flavoring ingredients. They add zest to your new cooking creations and make rapid weight loss easier.

Keep a plentiful supply of fresh fruits, but give special attention to oranges, apples, grapefruits and bananas. Use them individually or in combination as a salad.

Time Savers

Prepare soups, stews, and broths in large batches and store in plastic containers in the freezer. For smaller portions use ice cube trays to make cubes which can be stored in freezer bags. Use as many ice cubes as is necessary for portion requirements.

71

Exotic Stores

Almost every community across the United States has some kind of oriental grocery. Make it a habit to visit one in your community. All carry a wide variety of delicious oriental vegetables like bok choy, Chinese broccoli, Chinese cabbage, etc. These can be mixed with other recipes or developed according to your own tastes into creative new experiments.

Oriental groceries are also an excellent source for black mushrooms, fresh chiles, black beans, fresh ginger and probably some of the best fresh garlic available in your community. For the oriental grocery nearest you, look in the Yellow Pages under Oriental Grocery.

Health Food Stores

Introduce yourself to your local health food store. Even if you don't go along with the health food philosophy one hundred per cent, these stores provide many excellent ingredients for the BHMD which are usually unavailable in supermarkets. (See Shopping List.)

Cooking Tools

Most of the versatile techniques and savory menus on the BHMD can be prepared with the kitchen equipment that is probably already in your kitchen. A good blender, some non-stick frying pans, and an assortment of containers for dry and cold storage make up the most important part of the necessary accessories. But some equipment you may not have. The following is a list of the equipment that I've found most useful for the BHMD:

- *Cheesecloth*–for straining stock, skimming fat, cooking with spices, making low-cal cheeses.

- *Vegetable steaming basket*–useful for steaming all kinds of vegetables and fish.

- *Wire whisks*–perfect for whipping egg whites into a frothy substitute for dishes that usually call for yolks.

- *Garlic press*–makes fresh garlic easy to use and eliminates the need for garlic salts with their annoying aftertastes. Also good for crushing

72

ginger in low-cal, low-fat Chinese dishes.

- *Small scale*–for the most accurate measurement of meats and other portions that are measured by weight.
- *Non-stick sauce pans, small, medium and large*–You may also want to invest in a *non-stick cookie sheet*—great for baking, making oven-fried potatoes and eggplant, and reheating left-overs.
- *Wok*–a wonderful Chinese invention for cooking all kinds of vegetables and obtaining that crisp, stir-fried effect without oil. It's also great for use in poaching and steaming.

These are only the basics. If your kitchen is already stocked with other baking equipment, frying pans, graters, ladles, spatulas and the other common kitchen accessories you should be ready to begin. If it is not, you should make a list as you're preparing these recipes and add accessories to your kitchen as needed.

Such new gadgetry as microwave ovens, crockpots, food processors and juicers are handy but not necessary. Anyone with the basic kitchen tools and some kind of blender should be able to practice the BHMD.

Shopping

Good dieting should begin in the supermarket and health food store. You must learn to resist the responses programmed by advertising. Don't pick up the processed and fattening foods that tempt you. Remember, it's easier to resist those diet-breakers while they're still on the supermarket shelf than when they sit on your kitchen counter.

And before you set out from the house be sure you're not famished. Did you know that people who shop on a full stomach purchase between 10 and 20% less groceries than when they shop hungry? You'll be better able to resist the sugar-coated products if you always shop following a meal.

Also, shop only from a prepared list. A list helps in meal planning and learning about nutrition. It is part of your new eating behavior and helps develop the pattern that keeps you slim.

Shop first for produce. Let your shopping cart be your stomach and load up on fresh fruit and vegetables. Like your stomach, when your cart is full there is less chance of stuffing it with impulse items.

(The following items apply to all phases of the BHMD. Use this list in conjunction with BHMD daily menus and recipe plans.)

SHOPPING LIST

Dairy

Skim milk
Non-fat milk/powder
Cultured non-fat buttermilk powder
Non-fat buttermilk
Farmers, pot or hoop cheese (these are the same but may have different
 names depending on your part of the country)
Non-fat yogurt (if you can find it)
Low-fat yogurt (used sparingly as a substitute for non-fat)
99.5% fat-free cottage cheese
Parmesan cheese, grated
Eggs (no substitutes, though you'll only use the whites)

Pasta

Whole-wheat spaghetti
Whole-wheat macaroni
Egg-free noodles
Whole-wheat lasagne noodles

Breads

7-grains bread
Whole-wheat pita bread
Locally baked whole-wheat bread

Fruits

Apples
Oranges
Bananas
Grapes (limited)
Peaches
Pears

Cereals

Bran flakes
Grape-Nuts
Old fashioned rolled oats

Vegetables (Fresh)

Green (bell) peppers
Red (bell) peppers
Onions
Tomatoes
Romaine lettuce
Radishes
Celery
Carrots
Zucchini
Yellow squash
Sweet potatoes
Turnips
Rutabagas
Asparagus
Beets
Cucumbers
Chives

Spinach
Alfalfa sprouts
Beansprouts (will go bad if not
    used in 2-3 days)
Mushrooms
Squash – crooked
                butternut
                acorn
Fresh horseradish
Cabbage
Dried black mushrooms
Green Peas in pod

Eggplant
Parsley
Potatoes
Watercress
Fresh ginger
Fresh garlic

Note: If canned vegetables are used, be sure to buy the unsalted variety.

Grains

Barley
Rye flour
Whole wheat Durham flour
Buckwheat flour
Corn meal
Whole wheat pastry flour
Brown rice
Wild rice
Popcorn
Walnuts
Pine-nuts

Beans

Great Northern white beans
Black beans
Kidney beans
Navy beans
Peas
Small white beans
Lentils
Pinto beans
Garbanzo beans

Spices

Oregano	Cayenne pepper
Basil	Celery seeds
Thyme	Cinnamon
Marjoram	Cloves
Rosemary	Coriander
Bay leaves	Curry powder
Garlic powder	Ground cumin
Onion powder	Dillweed
Anise	Horseradish (powdered)
Dill seed	Mace
Dry mustard	Nutmeg
White vinegar	Paprika
Low-salt soy sauce	Parsley
Fresh garlic	Pepper (white/black)
Ginger powder	Vanilla extract
Yeast	Almond extract
Chili powder (without salt)	Bouillon (beef or chicken)
Cardamon	

Miscellaneous

Cheesecloth
3 non-stick saucepans – small, medium and large
Non-stick baking pan
Non-stick cupcake tin
PAM or other non-stick vegetable spray (limited use)

Health Food Stores

Many of the spices, grains, vitamins and some vegetables found in health food stores and food co-ops are of higher quality because these stores buy with greater nutritional consciousness than some of the supermarket chains. You may need to package and weigh the product yourself, but it's fun and consumes some of the time that you might be tempted to spend buying higher fat content foods in your local supermarket.

Here is a list of your best buys in a health food store:

Low-fat yogurt
Buckwheat flour
Whole wheat flour
Rice flour
Millet
Whole wheat pastry flour
Barley
Brown rice
7-grains bread
Rye flour
Whole rye seeds
Whole wheat pasta
All spices
Nutmeg (whole)
Arrowroot
Cloves

CHAPTER TWELVE:

HINTS FOR THE THIN CUISINE

LA TECHNIQUE

The following hints are designed to save you time and money, as well as to perk up your dishes with handy – and some quite ingenious! – ideas.

- *Baked potatoes*–rebake cold bake potatoes in 350° oven after first dipping in hot water. They will taste like new.
- *Bananas*–mash and freeze for later use when bananas show signs of going bad. Frozen bananas also make delicious low calorie popsicles. To keep bananas from darkening, simply dip in lemon juice.
- *Basil*–an excellent companion herb for tomatoes in any combination, in salad, tomato sauce, etc.
- *Blueberries*–wonderful additions to any fruit salad. Freeze in the basket just as they are. Do not wash. Wrap in foil or plastic wrap and they will keep their color and shape. Partially defrost frozen blueberries for use in muffins or pancakes. That way they won't blend in the cooking.
- *Browning*–to seal in the flavor and juices in roasts, fish, and chicken, brown by placing them under a hot broiler. While browning this way be

sure to baste with some liquid (broth, soup, water, etc.) for the juiciest effects.

- *Cabbage*–wash and dry a head of cabbage with paper toweling, then wrap in a plastic bag and freeze. When defrosted, the leaves are limp and easy to remove and handle. Perfect for stuffed cabbage. You won't have to boil cabbage again.
- *Carrots*–drop carrots in boiling water for 5 minutes, then drop them in cold water. The skins slip right off.
- *Cheese*–only use the cheese as described in the BHMD. Don't make the mistake that most dieters make. Cheese is actually more fattening than animal protein. Caloriewise, you're better off with the same amount of skinless white chicken, lean beef, or tuna.
- *Chicken*–the best way to debone and defat chicken is with a pair of ordinary kitchen scissors. It takes less time without the clumsy problem of using a knife.
- *Chiles*–whenever possible try and use fresh chiles when they're available. Char and remove the skins by impaling them on a fork and turning them over a gas flame. When the skin shows a black, burnt quality, they're ready to be skinned.
- *Chinese vegetables*–place leftover water chestnuts and bamboo shoots in a jar filled with water. Change every 2 or 3 days and they keep for weeks. Use your wok as a steamer. Simply take a rack from the oven and lay it over the wok. Boil water and steam-cook a delicious vegetable. Use soy sauce instead of oil and butter to brown vegetables.
- *Chives*–store chives in freezer, grating only enough for use each time; return the remainder to freezer. Tastes the same as when freshly chopped.
- *Coriander*–sometimes known as Chinese parsley or cilantro. Buy this parsley-like plant with the roots attached. To preserve it up to three weeks: Place it in an upright container of cold water and cover leaves with a plastic bag which is secured with a rubberband. Store in refrigerator, remove deteriorating leaves, and change the water every few days. To freeze, blend it with a little water and freeze as ice cubes. It's delicious in soups and vegetable stews.
- *Cornstarch*–always use cornstarch instead of flour in thickeners and save half the calories. The two are about equal in calories, but you need only half as much cornstarch.

- *Eggplant*–a good rule of thumb: If eggplant is cooked for a short time, peel the skin. If cooked longer, peeling isn't necessary. To rid it of bitterness, drop into salted water as you peel it. Pat it dry, and it's ready. For short time cooking with eggplant peel the skin.

- *Fat*–the best method for removing fat from soups and stews is to refrigerate it until the fat hardens on the top. If you don't have time for refrigeration you can strain off the fat in soups and broths by pouring them through several layers of cheesecloth.

- *Fish*–the yellow perch, along with the blue pike perch, yellow pike perch, and saugar have delicious, firm white meat with the lowest calories. The walleye or yellow pike is actually a perch. One hundred calories per 4 oz.

  Watch out for more fatty fish: salmon, swordfish, sardines, and pompano.

  The most succulent suggestion for fish lovers is trout. The rainbow, or salmon trout are the larger most useful members of this tempting, low-calorie dish. Calories: 115 per 4 oz. serving.

  Red Snapper, in my judgment, calorie for calorie, tastes the best on the BHMD. Calories: 105.

- *Fruits*–combine different varieties of fruit for fruit cups, using halved and hollowed melon or orange as cups. Garnish with such combinations as mint or cinnamon or berries; orange wedges and thawed frozen berries with a dash of lemon juice; banana and apple slices. Use your imagination.

- *Garlic*–a most versatile ingredient in the BHMD. It should be purchased in large quantities. Garlic cloves can be kept in the freezer. When ready to use just peel and chop before thawing.

  To remove skins before chopping, pound each clove with the side of a heavy knife, meat pounder, or a heavy bottle. The skin pops right off. Rub a clove of garlic over the inside surface of salad bowls prior to use. For the best garlic bread: Toast bread, and when done rub fresh peeled whole garlic clove across the surface.

- *Ginger*–keep fresh ginger for months in refrigerator. After cleaning, cut up or chop ginger and immerse in screw-top jar of sherry or vodka. To make a delightful iced ginger tea just boil the ginger root about 5 minutes, strain and pour over cracked ice.

- *Glazes*–make a delicious glaze for vegetables, chicken and fish by mixing apple juice and cornstarch in saucepan for a base. Other flavorings such as orange rind, lemon rind, curry, ginger, cinnamon, etc. may be added to achieve different flavors. Mix until smooth, and then heat until mixture thickens. Apply to desired foods as needed.

- *Gravy*–start with fat-free stock, season to taste (basil, oregano, garlic). Use arrowroot for clear sauces and cornstarch for creamier effects. Dash of low-salt soy will give "brown" look and skim milk a white creamy look.

- *Green peppers*–make attractive hors d'oeuvres by converting a large green pepper into a cask for appetizer diet dips. Cut off top, clear pepper inside of ribs and seeds, then fill with your choice of spicy low calorie dips. For final touch, place on a serving dish covered with bed of lettuce garnished on side with radish rosettes and cucumber slices. Remember, the better it looks the better it will taste!

- *Lemons*–look for lemons with the smoothest, thinnest skin. They have the most juice and best flavor.

- *Mushrooms*–to avoid waterlogged mushrooms simply rinse them quickly under cold running water. For sautes, pat mushrooms dry with paper towels. Store mushrooms in a brown paper bag in the refrigerator to prevent deterioration caused by plastic bags.

- *Okra*–as any of my southern patients tell me, okra makes a wonderful thickener for vegetable soups and stews.

- *Pineapple*–parboil fresh pineapple before using in a gelatin dish. In its fresh form it prevents gelatin from setting.

- *Poaching*–this simple technique seals in the juices in chicken and fish. Poaching is perfect for preparing chicken for salads, casseroles, and sandwiches. Heat poaching liquid in a pot or pan until the liquid rolls. Add the chicken or fish and cook for 10 to 15 minutes just below boiling.

    At no point should the liquid boil again or the meat will toughen.

    For fish, first wrap in cheesecloth before poaching to keep fish together. Add spices or wines to your water-based poaching liquid to enliven fish and chicken flavors.

- *Potatoes*–turn the much-maligned potato into an exciting and versatile additon to the BHMD. It is one of the tastiest, most nourishing and most filling of the low-calorie snacks. Keep baked potatoes in refrigerator and use with low-cal dips as a snack or slice and lay thin pieces on a cookie sheet, place in oven or under broiler until the potatoes look "fried." They're just as good as fried without the grease and calories.

- *Sauerkraut*–if it's too sour, drain and soak it in a large pot of cold water for 5 to 10 minutes. Stir it a little and drain.

- *Sauteing*–liquids like broths, soups, even water, can be used for excellent sauteing results. Just bring liquid to a boil in the bottom of pan and add vegetables, fish, or chicken.

- *Seasonings*–use seasonings as generously as your palate desires. They have no calories. Vinegars, mustards, horseradish, and lemon juice add delicious piquant flavor to vegetables, fish, chicken and beef. Curry, ground chili, cumin, and of course garlic, add delicious flavors to stews, soups, vegetable dips, and main courses. And nothing quite brings out the natural sweetness in many salads, fruits, and desserts like cinnamon.

- *Spaghetti*–to reheat whole-grain spaghetti run it under hot tap water in the strainer while shaking it vigorously.

- *Spices*–when using bay leaves or other such herbs that don't dissolve in soups and stews, place them in a tea ball for easy removal. Or, use a toothpick to skewer similar kinds of herbs. Makes it easier to spot them. For recipes that call for many spices, cook a day ahead allowing the flavors to "marry."

- *Sweetening*–cooking with carrots in soups, stews, and sauces adds sweetness. Apple juice and orange juice make delicious natural sweeteners for recipes that otherwise would call for a tablespoon or two of sugar. Each kind of juice is best with particular kinds of dishes. Experiment to see which satisfy your own taste. Cinnamon, nutmeg, vanilla, almond extract can be used liberally as sweetening substitutes.

- *Thickeners*–the best agents for creating thick creamy effects in soups, stews and especially sauces are arrowroot (available in health food stores) and cornstarch. Arrowroot leaves a transparent effect while cornstarch leaves a more cloudy one.

   To use, first make a thin paste of cornstarch or arrowroot. For cornstarch, add while the liquid is simmering, add slowly while stirring. For arrowroot, add just after liquid is removed from heat. Return to heat and stir until desired thickness is achieved.

- *Tomato juice*–enhance the taste of an ordinary 46 oz. can of tomato juice by first pouring it into a refrigerator bottle. Then add 1 green onion and 1 stalk celery cut into small pieces. It's delicious.

- *Tortillas*–corn tortillas, not flour, are excellent sources of vitamins and fiber. They're wonderful substitutes for breads and can be used to make tacos rich with vegetables, chile sauce, and small amounts of beans and meat for flavoring.

Tortillas can be heated easily without frying or placing in the oven by simply placing the cold or frozen tortilla directly over the flame on your stove. Turn the tortilla briskly until it is soft and hot. It's ready to eat.

- *Vinegar*–create your own special vinegar flavors for seasonings and marinades. Add the ingredients to the vinegar and let stand at room temperature for at least 1 week before using. Tarragon, dill, celery are excellent flavors for white vinegar. Add 12 fresh or unsweetened frozen raspberries to 2 cups red wine vinegar and create an exciting raspberry vinegar excellent for salads and as a fish marinade.

CHAPTER THIRTEEN:

CHEATING ON THE BHMD

DON'T FEEL GUILTY

When it comes to dieting we are all a bit larcenous at heart. We all feel that once in a while we can pull the wool over our own eyes and gorge on a candy bar or pastry. We make a small raid on the local pizza parlor, smothering our system with grease, and return home as if we have just committed the perfect crime. And also we know, to our grief, the consequences of such splurges: the dismay over our weakness.

Of course, the last thing I wish to do is to encourage cheating on the diet. But in my experience with the BHMD I have noticed that dieting is frequently as much a psychological as a physical discipline. What I have learned is that the guilty emotions of the occasional diet-breaker actually do more harm than the transgression itself.

Guilt causes frustration, which causes depression, which makes you want to give up the diet. Therefore, I tell my patients, "If you must cheat, do it. Go at it and have done with it. But *don't feel guilty.*"

The extraordinary thing is, it works!

My patients sometimes cheat but they stick to the diet. Their occasional weakness for a forbidden item does not interfere with their determination to follow the BHMD. That's because they do not allow themselves to be assailed by self-reproach. They do not feel guilty because they cheat according to certain principles that are part of the BHMD program. If once in a while they lapse, they nevertheless continue cheerfully with the plan as if nothing had happened.

It goes without saying that the BHMD only permits cheating. *By no means does it recommend departures from the basic rules.* The BHMD realizes that skipping a day of dieting won't make a great deal of difference in the long run. However, if you want to shed weight rapidly you must control your cheating to a minimum. You are advised that on the "Plunge" any departure will slow your rapid weight loss.

HOW MUCH CAN YOU CHEAT?

I divide cheating on the diet between felonies and misdemeanors. Certain foods high in fats and cholesterol are felonies. Others of lighter consequence to your waistline, are misdemeanors. With the Cheating Chart, you can be the judge in assessing the damages of the violation.

As a general principle, however, you can stay clear of the law by cheating in acordance with the BHMD guidelines. For example, if you're going to cheat by eating more of an entree, say a pasta dish, then try and indulge in whole-wheat pasta. It makes sense to break the rules with a food that is high in Complex Carbohydrates rather than with a creamy butter sauce, rich in fats and cholesterol.

The same goes for sweets, the most common area of cheating. If you are overwhelmed by a sweet tooth, indulge yourself with fruit salad or a spoonful of honey and low-fat yogurt. A snack high in Complex Carbohydrates and some simple sugars is not nearly as bad as a French pastry, loaded with butter, egg yolks and cream

The Cheating Chart shows the foods you are most likely to overindulge in while following the BHMD. Each of these contains more protein, sugar, fats—and calories!—than you need. The calorie values are given. But you are advised that on the "Plunge" cheating beyond 350 calories a week will wreck your rapid weight-loss goal. Cheating by more than 700 calories a week on the "Everyday" weight loss will also throw you off.

If you *must* cheat, try to use elements that add flavor to high-vegetable, low-fat meals. For instance: a little wine to flavor a stew, a tablespoon or two of cheese for some pasta, a teaspoonful of sesame oil for a Chinese vegetable salad.

85

Cheating Chart

Food	Calories	Maximum Amt. Plunge[1]	Maximum Amt. Everyday[1]
Egg Yolks* 1	60	6	12
Oils* 1 T.	120	9 t.	18 t.
Butter* 1 T.	100	7 t.	14 t.
Hard Cheeses* 1 T.	23	15 T.	30 T.
Soft Cheeses* 1 oz.	100	3½ oz.	7 oz.

Ice Cream*

10% fat, ½ c.	129	1½ c.	3 c.
12% fat, ½ c.	138	1¼ c.	2½ c.
Rich 16% fat, ½ c.	165	1 c.	2 c.
Sugar come	37	1	2
Waffle cone	19	1	2
Bar, chocolate coated, 3 oz.	162	2	4
Ice milk, hardened 5.1% fat, ½ c.	100	3.5 c.	7 c.
Pie 4⅛″ arc (1/6 of 8″ pie)	282	1	2
Cookie 1 oz.	120	3	6

Cake

Cupcake without icing (2¾″ diameter)	116	3	6
Cupcake with chocolate icing (2¾″ diam.)	172	2	4
Angelfood without icing 3½ oz.	269	1	2

Cooking Liquors
Wines, 4 oz.

Red and white, 12-12½% alcohol	400	4 oz.	8 oz.

Fruit juices (unsweetened)

Apple 1 c.	117	3.5 c.	7 c.
Grape 1 c.	150	2⅓ c.	4⅔ c.
Lemon 1 c.	61	5.5 c.	11 c.
Orange 1 c.	112	3.5 c.	7 c.
Pineapple 1 c.	138	2⅓ c.	4⅔ c.
Prune 1 c.	197	1.5 c.	3 c.
Tomato 1 c.	46	7 c.	14 c.
V-8 1 c.	35	10 c.	20 c.

Meat*
4 oz.

	350	4 oz.	8 oz.

*These foods are not only high in calories but also contain fats and cholesterol which should generally be avoided by dieters and non-dieters alike.

[1]Consumption of this amount exhausts all cheating for the whole week.

CHAPTER FOURTEEN:

RECIPES FOR THE THIN CUISINE

LOW-CAL COOKING

The most important part of an effective diet are the recipes. Thus far you have learned the theory behind the BHMD—the how and why of its safe and speedy weight-loss program. Now you are going to transform your kitchen into the *Thin Cuisine*. From *thinking* slim, you'll be *cooking* slim.

I've long realized that if people are to shed weight rapidly and maintain their new figure, they must enjoy what they eat. Ultimately, if their diet is to be a success and remain a permanent part of their lives, they have to learn to prepare dishes that are as good as or better than the ones they're replacing. That's why in developing the BHMD menus I've been guided by three standards: the recipes must be simple, practical, and—above all—tasty.

Once you have mastered the simple cooking elements you will be astonished that "diet food" can be so asolutely delicious. The BHMD recipes incorporate imaginative new ways of preparing dishes that are nothing less than gastronomic achievements.

The Thin Cuisine is meant to encourage a new way of cooking in order to change your eating patterns. As such it is as much a learning experience as it is a prescription for weight loss and health.

While practicing the Thin Cuisine you will obtain a flair for substituting low-cal ingredients for fats, oils and sugars. These substitutions are calculated to please your palate just as much as the pound-padding ingredients they are replacing. You will learn to make dishes low in animal protein without losing the zesty flavors which meats, poultry and fish impart to meals. And you will be surprised to see how fast your high-animal protein and high-fat eating habits become ancient history. For your lowered dependence on animal protein will soon become just as satisfying as your former high intake of this product.

Thus, innovative ideas on spicing, creative methods of mixing, and all kinds of delicious combinations will become part of your dazzling new cooking techniques. At the same time, however, you are absorbing the discipline vital to making the Thin Cuisine a permanent fixture.

By using the shopping information you become accustomed to allocating your resources. By following the recipes you automatically learn to diminish fats and oils in your cooking. By being encouraged to think creatively you discover new ways of making vegetables and grains taste delicious. The recipes teach you the planning so necessary to rational eating.

If you follow the BHMD menus meal-planning becomes part of your daily routine. Thus, you think of salads and soups in addition to the entree. For the entree your first thoughts will be how to reduce the beef components or other high-fat meats. You'll think of them as flavoring agents to mix with vegetables, stews, casseroles and salads. And once you've attained this point in meal-planning you've come a long way in modifying your eating behavior.

The Thin Cuisine is full of surprises, and not long after you've come down to your desired weight you will be continually discovering new ideas for the preparation of dishes other than those described in the BHMD. That's when your food consumption pattern has permanently changed and you will never again be confronted by the problem of being overweight.

Before you enter on your new adventure in cooking, remember that your dishes will be tastier and more nutritious if you use fresh and unprocessed ingredients. While it's true that many of these recipes can be prepared from canned or frozen goods, try to get fresh items always. Whenever possible use the whole grains instead of refined ones. The taste and texture of whole grains is better for you.

Bon Appetit!

CHAPTER FIFTEEN:

THE PLUNGE:
RAPID WEIGHT LOSS

HERE WE GO!

Many of you have gone through the BHMD book and have come back to start with this section. You decided not to shilly-shally. You want to lose weight fast. Maybe you feel it's now or never. Maybe your clothes no longer fit. Perhaps you have your hopes pinned on a new romance. You want to rekindle the marital flame. You're going for a job where a trim appearance is considered an asset. Whatever the reason may be, you've decided to shed weight rapidly. You're determined to take the "Plunge."

Something irrevocable and final seems to be connected with that word "Plunge." But let me hasten to assure you it is not at all as forbidding as it seems. The discipline on this segment is a little more rigorous than on the other parts of the BHMD, the Everyday and Maintenance weight loss. But if you abide by the rules you will find no difficulty in losing ten-to-twelve pounds in two weeks in the safest and most efficient manner possible.

What makes the "Plunge" rather less unnerving than it sounds is the special care with which the accompanying menus have been selected. They have been particularly chosen to make speedy fat-shedding a delight to the palate and a filling satisfaction to the stomach. In fact, the strictest regimen of the BHMD is unlike any other diet in that, with a few slight changes or additions for non-dieters, it provides meals which the whole family can enjoy. So while you are 'plunging,' other members of the family will benefit from the sound nutrition you are giving them in their less strictly constituted portions of the same meal.

WHAT THE "PLUNGE" DOES:

1. It promotes rapid weight loss without killing yourself.
2. It restores nutritional sanity.
3. It reduces stress.
4. It provides extremely tasty, inexpensive, and low-calorie menus and recipes that set the stage for a new way of eating.
5. It lowers high blood pressure and controls blood sugar problems.
6. It regulates normal bowel function.
7. It teaches simple new dieting behavior that curbs appetite.
8. It conditions you into good health.

POINTERS FOR PLUNGING

If you're the typical American on a high-protein, high-fat, high-cholesterol diet then your body is out of balance with nature. It should therefore be additionally gratifying to know that while you are "plunging" into the world of Complex Carbohydrates, you are not just losing fat speedily: you are also putting yourself back in balance with the way man was intended to eat.

The BHMD program of Complex Carbohydrates provides you with natural vitamins, as well as with the fiber so often missing from the typical American diet of processed foods and denuded grains. *Fiber may be supplemented in the form of bran if you continue to experience bowel problems while on the BHMD. Starting with one or two tablespoons of unprocessed wheat bran flakes added daily to your diet, the bran can be added to blender drinks, casseroles, meat loaves, etc.*

While on the Plunge, you'll learn to eat more vegetables, whole grains and citrus fruits. The BHMD shows you that vegetables need not taste like "rabbit food." It teaches you how to prepare vegetables and meats.

In addition to following the general rules of the BHMD, try and adopt these dietary patterns:

- Always carry a baggie with raw vegetables and a piece of fresh fruit when you go out and don't expect to have a meal soon. Never let yourself get too hungry.
- Eat raw and cooked fresh vegetables every day.
- In spicing and seasoning, go by taste preference rather than the recipe instruction.
- Make a special effort to eat whole-grain foods and beans in place of animal protein foods.
- Eat fresh fruits, preferably citrus fruits and apples, in place of all of the sugary snacks that play havoc with the typical diet.
- Once you've lost weight and obtained a stable weight level, keep a careful eye on calories and try to maintain your new Complex Carbohydrate, low-fat approach to eating. Many people experience such an overall rejuvenation on the BHMD that controlling their new weight level becomes easier than ever before.

DO DRINK PLENTY OF WATER

You need water. Drink 6 to 8 glasses a day.

Coffee and Coke contain caffeine, which is a stressor. Caffeine triggers off the fight or flight response of your body to stress. Sodas are not really drinks. They are better described as "20 teaspoons of sugar suspended in colored water."

Fruit juices are harmful because food processors "refine" out all the fiber, leaving only the sugar and color. (Fruit juice is OK if it is made from the *entire* fruit.)

Stick with water. Besides, the ability of a liquid to quench your thirst is in direct proportion to its water content.

PLUNGE RULES

1. *Get ready* for the Plunge the weekend before. "Psyche" yourself up for the step that is going to make such a momentous change in your life. Spend the weekend preparing the contents of the baggies, cutting up carrot sticks, celery, cauliflower, broccoli, etc. to take to work.

   You may also want to use a microwave to prepare a number of ready-to-eat meals for the rest of the week. It takes an average of one hour to fix a meal from the BHMD menu, no longer than the time for the ordinary high-fat, high-protein dinner. But you'll be one step ahead if you freeze soups and sauces, or if you keep your favorite beans or rice in a container in the refrigerator.

2. *Weighing yourself* can be an extremely frustrating experience. Don't weigh yourself every day. The daily weight variations due to water, bowel movements and other metabolic processes can be extremely misleading.

Weigh yourself twice a week. If you follow the Plunge diet you should average about a pound-and-a-half every other day. To slow down your weight loss, switch to the Everyday Program and you'll shed a couple of pounds weekly. For good health, stress-free feelings, and weight maintenance follow the Maintenance Program.

When the scale starts to return to its old levels simply switch back to the Plunge for a week or two and get yourself back into a pattern of healthy stress-free eating.

3. *Planning your meals* creates nutritional consciousness and reinforces rapid weight loss. Strictly adhere to the menus and recipes. Do not experiment or improvise. You'll be able to indulge your imagination more freely on the Everyday and Maintenance plans.

4. *Eating three full meals daily* prevents your going hungry. *Eat all day long.* Munch whenever you can. Always carry baggies with raw green pepper, cauliflower, broccoli, carrots, celery. Dip them in one of the BHMD dips. Or have a piece of fruit or some whole grain crackers. Have some vegetable and dip before meals to regulate appetite.

5. *Chewing* seems to be a forgotten practice these days. One of the things many of my dieting patients appear to have in common is fast eating. Slow down!

By slowing your food intake you'll do your body and your eating habits a favor. Give your stomach enough time to tell your brain that your appetite is satisfied. When you chew and swallow each mouthful slowly your body requires less food.

6. *Sticking* to the plan is your goal. Don't cheat!

When temptation strikes keep your jaws moving by munching on raw vegetables, but don't binge on foods that are bad for you. If you follow the BHMD instructions you'll lose weight rapidly, experience a new feeling of self-confidence and move closer to an entirely new way of eating.

7. *Sit down and slow down.* I can't reiterate how important it is to slow down your eating and chew, chew, chew.

92

A related problem is that of the stand-up eater. *NEVER EAT WHILE STANDING.*

People eat standing up so as to avoid thinking about how much they are really eating. According to my experience with patients, I've learned that overeaters stand up near the refrigerator or over the kitchen sink to "sneak" food.

Sit down, slow down, trim down!

8. *Only use* the cheeses as described in the BHMD. Don't follow the mistake of most dieters. Cheese is actually more fattening than animal protein. Calorie-wise, you're better off with the same amount of skinless white chicken, lean beef, or tuna.

9. *Give yourself* a real boost by making your diet dinner something special. Set your table formally. Use your best china, silver and crystal. Make the meal look festive. You are celebrating the unveiling of a new slim and healthy appearance!

EQUIVALENTS BY VOLUME

(All measurements level)

1 quart	=	4 cups
1 cup	=	8 fluid ounces
	=	½ pint
	=	16 tablespoons
2 tablespoons	=	1 fluid ounce
1 tablespoon	=	3 teaspoons
1 pound regular butter of margarine	=	4 sticks
	=	2 cups
1 pound whipped butter or margarine	=	6 sticks
	=	2 8-ounce containers
	=	3 cups
1 pound (16 ounces)	=	453.6 grams
1 ounce	=	28.35 grams
3½ ounces	=	100 grams

THE PLUNGE

Here's the 14-day Plunge Program with menus and recipes designed to drop your weight by at least 10 pounds in two weeks. To continue losing weight at this pace just repeat the cycle. Read all of the menus before you start.

MONDAY MENU

Breakfast
　　½ grapefruit
　　½ c. whole grain cereal (my favorite is Scotch oatmeal,
　　　　other oatmeals are also good)
　　½ c. skim milk
　　tea (preferably Linden tea or one of the low-tannin, low-caffeine
　　　　teas. Most Chinese teas fit this description.)

Lunch
　　Rodeo Drive Cocktail
　　Tossed Salad
　　WIN-VIN Dressing
　　water with sliced lemon or Linden tea

Dinner
　　Baked Bass
　　steamed broccoli and carrots
　　Tossed Salad with WIN-VIN Dressing
　　small baked potato
　　1 apple

TUESDAY MENU

Breakfast
½ grapefruit
⅔ c. Shredded Wheat (bite size)
½ c. skim milk
tea

Lunch
Cottage Cheese Yogurt a la Palms
slice of whole wheat bread
tea or water

Dinner
Sunset Soup
Malibu Style Snapper
Salad with WIN-VIN dressing
steamed broccoli
Linden tea and/or mineral water

WEDNESDAY MENU

Breakfast
3 oz. Oatmeal
½ c. skim milk (optional)
½ orange
tea

Lunch
Cold Cucumber-Spinach Garbo
1 slice toast
Raw Vegetables
Bedford (No Fat) Salad Dressing
tea or mineral water

Dinner
Ratatouille (2 cups)
Salad with WIN-VIN dressing
Wilshire Salad with Vanilla Mock Sour Cream
tea and/or mineral water

THURSDAY MENU

Breakfast
      3 oz. oatmeal
      ¼ grapefruit or ¼ papaya
      one glass of water
      tea

Lunch
      Chicken Fried Rice
      1 apple
      Club Soda or Mineral water with lemon

Dinner
      Tangy Tuna/The Maid's Night Out
      steamed vegetables (broccoli, brussel sprouts, mushrooms)
      tea and/or mineral water

FRIDAY MENU

Breakfast
      Quick Breakfast Drink

Lunch
      Southern Soup
      Cucumber-Yogurt Salad (one cup)
      tea or water

Dinner
      Papas y Pollo (Potato & Chicken)
      lots of steamed green beans and broccoli
      lettuce and tomatoes*
      tea and/or water

*For lettuce and tomato salads in BHMD program, use 1 or 2 Tablespoons of your choice of dressing from Chapter Seventeen.

SATURDAY MENU

Breakfast
½ grapefruit
½ papaya
tea and a glass of water

Lunch
Szechuan Salad
tea

Dinner
Broiled Sole
lettuce and tomato salad with Herb Vinegar Dressing
L.A. Fruit Cup

SUNDAY MENU

Breakfast
½ grapefruit
½ c. oatmeal
tea

Lunch
Falafel Sandwich with Tomato Yogurt Sauce

Dinner
4 oz. roast turkey or chicken (white meat, skin and visible fat
removed before cooking)
steamed vegetables (broccoli, brussel sprouts, green beans – ad
lib)
lettuce and tomato salad with choice of dressing

MONDAY MENU

Breakfast
Bran Muffin
Cran-Orange Drink

Lunch
Cukes in Yogurt
1 slice bread or Kavli crackers
Bean Sprout Coleslaw

Dinner
Mediterranean Meat Loaf
Gazpacho
Tabouli Salad
Baked Apple

TUESDAY MENU

Breakfast
Quick Breakfast Drink

Lunch
Tangy Tuna
lettuce wedge or 4 Romaine leaves
4 Kavli crackers
small apple

Dinner
Broiled Herb Chicken
Spiced Carrots
String Bean Salad
Orange Fruit Cups

WEDNESDAY MENU

Breakfast
    Bran Muffin
    Strawberry Yogurt

Lunch
    Ratatouille
    Pear

Dinner
    Veal Scallopini Marsala
    Wild Rice and Mushrooms
    Asparagus with Lemon-Parsley Sauce
    Herb Tomatoes Parmigiano
    Sweet Potato Boat

THURSDAY MENU

Breakfast
    Marina del Egg
    ½ grapefruit

Lunch
    Tuna Salad
    4 Ry-Crisp Crackers

Dinner
    Arroz Con Pollo (Rice with Chicken)
    Zucchini Espanola
    Lettuce and tomato salad

FRIDAY MENU

Breakfast
    Egg Omelet
    Apple Shake

Lunch
    Spinach and Mushroom Salad
    Fresh Garden Soup
    apple, banana

Dinner
    Steak
    Brown Rice
    Fresh Garden Soup
    Stuffed Zucchini
    Orange Fruit Cup

SATURDAY MENU

Breakfast
    Tomato Cocktail
    ½ grapefruit
    4 Potato Pancakes

Lunch
    Vegetable Cream Soup
    Stuffed Zucchini

Dinner
    Vegetable Cream Soup
    Curried Beef
    Steamed Eggplant
    Frozen Banana

SUNDAY MENU

Brunch
    Oven "Fried" Potatoes
    Cheese-Zucchini Quiche
    Tomato Salad
    1 slice toast
    Mandarin Pudding

Dinner
    Baked Brown Rice with Mushrooms
    Tandoori Chicken
    steamed broccoli
    Glazed Yams

MONDAY RECIPES

Breakfast

Oatmeal

1 c. oatmeal (try the different varieties at your favorite health food store or other store that sells oatmeal unpackaged, or Old Fashioned Oats)

Boil 2 cups of water and stir in the oatmeal, cover and cook it slowly over a low heat. I like it somewhat gritty (the Scotch Oatmeal, etc.) so I cook it only 10 minutes. For others 12-15 minutes may be better. Stir a bit near the end of the time. Sprinkle lightly with cinnamon. Makes 3 cups.

Lunch

Rodeo Drive Cocktail

2 c. pineapple juice, unsweetened
1 c. packed watercress leaves without stems

2 t. lime or lemon juice
1 c. ice, cracked

Place all the ingredients in a blender and blend until nice and frothy. Makes 4 six ounce servings.

Tossed Salad

Combine 2 cups of shredded lettuce (Romaine, Salad Bowl, Boston or Red Leaf), 4-5 radishes, ½ green pepper and ½ cucumber. Dice one medium tomato. Add ½ cup of alfalfa sprouts and 1 cup of shredded carrot. Toss to mix. Serves 1.

WIN-VIN Dressing

Mix one cup of wine or cider vinegar with one cup of water and add:
½ t. oregano
½ t. basil
¼ t. dry mustard
¼ t. rosemary
3 t. dried parsley flakes
1 clove garlic, minced finely or crushed
¼ c. apple juice, unsweetened
¼ c. lemon juice

Mix all ingredients and shake well before using. Keeps in refrigerator for weeks; flavor enhanced with time.

Dinner

Baked Bass

1 lb. sea bass or halibut
2 medium lemons, sliced
2 medium onions, thinly sliced
3 cloves garlic, minced
   or crushed
1 c. celery, finely chopped

1 small eggplant, diced ½″
1 small can tomato paste with
   water to make it 1¼ cups
1 t. cumin powder
1 large tomato, sliced

Preheat oven to 350°. Dry saute onions and garlic in heavy pan. Add celery, eggplant, tomato paste, water and spices. Simmer 5 minutes. Transfer to oven-proof baking dish. Spread half of the sauce (see below) over the vegetables and spices. Put in the fish and cover it with the remaining sauce, lemon and tomato slices. Cover and bake for 20 minutes. Uncover, continue baking for 5 minutes.

Sauce for Fish

2 t. lemon juice
2 t. mustard
2 t. horseradish

¼ t. white pepper
pinch paprika

Serves 4.

TUESDAY RECIPES

Lunch

Cottage Cheese Yogurt a la Palms

½ c. low fat, low sodium
cottage cheese

½ c. plain low fat yogurt
½ t. chopped dill

Mix cottage cheese and yogurt and add desired amounts of: cucumbers, radishes, green peppers. Add chopped dill. Sprinkle with fresh ground pepper (optional). Serves 1.

Dinner

Sunset Soup

10 whole canned tomatoes,
quartered
1 medium onion, diced
½ medium lemon, sliced
2 cloves garlic, crushed
½ c. each shredded carrots,
green peppers and cabbage

10 sprigs parsley
1 bay leaf
1 t. peppercorn, ground
1 T. mock sour cream (optional)
4 c. water
dash of allspice

Put the parsley, bay leaf, peppercorn, tomatoes, onion, lemon, garlic and allspice into a large pot. Add 4 cups of water and bring to a boil. Reduce the heat and let simmer for 30 minutes. Puree in blender. Return to pot and bring to medium heat. Stir in the carrots, green peppers, and cabbage. Simmer until carrots are tender. Serve hot. Optional: add one tablespoon Mock Sour Cream. See following recipe. Serves 4.

Mock Sour Cream

Blend equal parts of hoop cheese and skim milk to the desired consistency. (Hoop cheese, farmers and pot cheese – synonymous).

Malibu Style Snapper

1½ lbs. Red Snapper, filet	2 t. orange peel, grated
¼ c. onion, freshly grated	¼ t. nutmeg
2 t. orange juice	1 medium lemon, sliced
2 t. lemon juice	

Thaw filets, if frozen, and cut the fish into six portions. Place in a single layer, skin side down in a baking dish (approx. 12" x 8"). Combine the onions, orange and lemon juice and orange peel. Pour over the fish. Cover and refrigerate for 30 minutes. Remove from refrigerator and sprinkle with nutmeg. Bake uncovered at 350° for 25-30 minutes, or until the fish flakes easily when tested with a fork. Garnish with lemon slices. Serves 6.

WEDNESDAY RECIPES

Breakfast

Oatmeal

⅓ c. rolled oats	¾ c. water
1 t. pine nuts	¼ t. cinnamon

Mix all the ingredients in a small saucepan and bring to a boil. Let simmer over a small flame for 5 minutes. You may add a little skim milk if desired. Serves 1.

Lunch

Cold Cucumber-Spinach Garbo

1 large cucumber, sliced	2 c. buttermilk
10 oz. fresh or frozen spinach	the juice of one lemon
(leaf or chopped)	healthy pinch each of cumin
3 medium green onions	powder, fresh ground
with tops, sliced	pepper and garlic powder

Cook the spinach in a pan with ½ cup water. Place in a good size bowl to cool. Add the cucumber, onion, buttermilk, lemon juice, garlic powder, pepper and cumin and stir. Chill before serving. Serves 5.

Raw Vegetables

carrots, sliced thin	celery, sliced thin
mushrooms, sliced thin	

(Eat all you like, see *STUFF FOR THE BAGGIE,* p. 140)

Bedford (No Fat) Salad Dressing

1 c. skim milk	1 small clove garlic,
1 t. cornstarch OR	minced or crushed
½ t. arrowroot	½ t.dry mustard powder
1 egg white	2 t. white vinegar

Combine skim milk and cornstarch in a container and shake. Pour into a deep pan and cook over low heat, stirring until thick. Remove from heat. Add garlic and dry mustard and return to heat. Add vinegar and beat until consistency is smooth. Beat egg white and fold into mixture. Chill.

Dinner

Ratatouille

1 medium eggplant, peeled and
   diced into ½" cubes
4 medium zucchini, cut
   into ¼" slices
2 medium green peppers, seeded
   and cut into 1" strips
5 medium tomatoes, peeled,
   seeded and chopped

2 medium onions, sliced thin
6 medium okra, cut in 1" strips
3 cloves garlic, freshly minced
1 t. basil
1 t. oregano
1 t. white pepper
½ t. thyme, dried
1 bay leaf
½ c. chicken broth or bouillon

In a Dutch oven dry saute the onions, pepper and garlic until the onion wilts. Add the bay leaf, thyme, basil, oregano, white pepper, and stir. Add all of the other ingredients, cover and cook over low heat for 25 minutes, until the vegetables are tender but crisp. Add ½ cup chicken bouillon, broth or water to render sauce if desired. Uncover the pot and cook for approximately 10 minutes longer over moderate heat, stirring until the desired consistency is reached. Serves 6.

The Wilshire Salad

3 medium apples, diced
   (Delicious, if in season)
1 c. celery, diced
1 medium orange, diced

¼ c. raisins
1 c. Vanilla Mock Sour Cream
1 medium lemon, juiced (fresh)
lettuce leaves

Sprinkle the lemon juice over the apples to prevent discoloration. Mix and toss apples, orange, celery, raisins, and vanilla mock sour cream. Arrange the salad attractively on the lettuce. Serves 3-4.

Vanilla Mock Sour Cream

½ skim milk   ½ t. vanilla extract
½ c. hoop cheese

Combine and blend to consistency of sour cream.

THURSDAY RECIPES

Lunch

Chicken Fried Rice

4 oz. diced chicken, cooked   ½ fresh garlic clove
½ c. cooked brown rice   2 whole green onions
3 T. soy sauce   ½ T. fresh ginger, finely chopped
    (salt-reduced kind)   ¼ c. chicken bouillon

Finely chop the whole green onions, separating the green chive from the white onion part. Saute the crushed garlic, ginger, and finely chopped white onion parts in chicken bouillon for 2-3 minutes. Bring to a high flame and add chicken. Cook for 2-3 minutes. Lower flame, simmer until chicken is tender. Add cooked brown rice. Toss until rice is coated with saute. Add soy sauce to taste. When hot, add the chopped green chives, toss and serve. Note: many vegetables can be steamed, finely chopped and mixed with this dish for even more delicious meals. Try broccoli, eggplant, and zucchini this way. May warm up next day in microwave or pan – just add fresh chives. Serves 1.

Dinner

Tangy Tuna/The Maid's Night Out

In a collander, gently rinse ½ can of tuna (water pack and low sodium) with water spray. Combine with lemon juice (as desired), gently mashing tuna with a fork. Add finely chopped vegetables from the unlimited vegetables list. Mix in a small amount of Spicy Lemon Dressing (See p. 188) and mock sour cream to the desired consistency. Serves 1.

FRIDAY RECIPES

Breakfast

Quick Breakfast Drink

Put in a blender:
½ c. skim milk
2 t. plain low fat yogurt

½ t. vanilla
½ banana (ripe), peach, or papaya (try a mango for a real treat)
½ t. cinnamon (or to taste)

Blend until smooth.

Lunch

Southern Soup

1 c. okra (fresh or frozen)	3 c. tomato juice
1 c. Chinese pea pods	1 t. basil, dried
2 c. cabbage, shredded	1 bay leaf
1 c. carrots, chopped	½ t. white pepper
½ c. onion, diced	½ t. cumin
½ c. celery, chopped	3 c. water

Mix the water and tomato juice and bring to a boil. Add all of the other ingredients except the okra. After boiling for 2-3 minutes, reduce the heat and simmer for approximately 1 hour. Add the okra and continue cooking for 15 minutes. Serves 6-8.

Cucumber-Yogurt Salad

2 large cucumbers	1 t. tops of green onions, chopped
1 c. yogurt, plain low-fat	¼ t. white pepper
1 t. lemon juice	½ t. cumin powder
1 t. parsley	½ t. Worcestershire sauce
1 t. chives	lettuce leaves

Cut the cucumbers in half lengthwise, scoop out the seeds, and cut into small slices horizontally. To the yogurt add the lemon juice, parsley, chives, green onion tops, white pepper, cumin and Worcestershire sauce. Add the cucumber slices, toss and chill for 30 minutes prior to serving. Serve one half to one cupful on the lettuce leaves. Serves 4-8.

Dinner

Papas y Pollo (Potatoes & Chicken)

1 small baked potato
2 oz. shredded chicken,
   cooked (fat and skin
   removed)

1 T. low-fat yogurt
2 T. red chile sauce*
1 green onion, finely chopped

After baking potato, let cool slightly and remove the skin. Place in 350° oven for 20 minutes until the outside is brown and crisp. While the potato is "frying" shred the chicken and chop green onion. When the potato is ready place it on a plate and firmly smash top. Place shredded chicken on top, and add salsa, green onion and yogurt. This is a very simple meal, delicious and very common in the southeastern part of Mexico. Serves 1.

*See Chapter Seventeen.

SATURDAY RECIPES

Lunch

Szechuan Salad

¼ c. beef bouillon broth
1 c. broccoli flowerets
½ sweet red bell pepper
½ c. sliced fresh mushrooms
4 T. white vinegar
2 T. soy sauce (salt reduced)
crushed, dried red peppers –
    to taste

½ garlic clove, crushed
¼ T. fresh ginger
2 oz. rare lean roast beef,
    julienned thinly
4 pcs. bamboo shoots
4 water chestnuts

In a large, non-stick skillet heat about ⅛ cup beef broth. Add broccoli and stir-fry until broccoli becomes tender but is still crisp (about 3 minutes). Transfer broccoli to a bowl. Stir-fry the sweet red pepper strips in the same pan over moderate heat for 1-2 minutes. Add more beef broth as needed. Transfer to the broccoli bowl. Do the same with the mushrooms and add cooked to broccoli-red pepper mix. In a small glass jar or container with top: mix vinegar, soy sauce, crushed garlic, crushed fresh ginger and crushed red pepper (to taste). Shake, then pour over the broccoli-red pepper-mushroom mixture. Toss gently. Add beef strips, water chestnuts and bamboo shoots to vegetable mixture and toss gently. Cover and refrigerate for 3 hours and serve as a luncheon salad or for dinner over a bed of brown rice (½ cup). Note: This can be made the night before also. The sauce becomes somewhat more flavorful if kept refrigerated for 24 hours. Serves 1-2.

Dinner

Broiled Sole

1 lb. filet of sole
¼ c. lemon juice
½ t. paprika

1 clove garlic, finely minced
    or crushed
3 T. parsley

Put the lemon juice into a bowl. Dip the fish into the juice, making sure both sides are coated. Mix the remaining ingredients and sprinkle onto both sides of the fish. Broil until a golden brown color. Serves 4.

Herb Vinegar Dressing

1 c. wine vinegar
¼ c. fresh dill or
½ t. dried dillweed
¼ c. snipped fresh chives

⅓ c. snipped fresh mint
1 clove garlic, finely chopped
¼ c. parsley

Combine all the ingredients. Let the dressing stay in the refrigerator for at least 4 days to get maximum flavor. Strain to remove herbs. Makes about 1¼ cups.

L.A. Fruit Cup

1 medium apple,
     cored and diced
1 medium orange,
     peeled and diced
1 medium peach,
     pitted and diced
1 medium banana,
     peeled and sliced

½ c. seedless grapes, halved
½ c. blueberries
2 t. walnuts, finely chopped
3 t. frozen orange juice
     concentrate
1 t. lemon (to taste)

Place the orange juice concentrate into a bowl and mix in the fruits. Chill.
Garnish each serving with a bit of the chopped walnuts. Serves 6.

SUNDAY RECIPES

Lunch

Falafel Sandwich with Tomato-Yogurt Sauce

Falafel mix:
2 oz. lean ground beef
½ c. pureed cooked
   garbanzo beans
1 egg white

¼ c. finely shredded
   white cabbage
½ t. ground cumin
1 small garlic clove, crushed
black pepper to taste

Mix all ingredients in a bowl and form tablespoon size patties. Fry in a non-stick skillet over medium heat until crispy on the outside.

Stuffing:
¼-½ c. shredded lettuce
¼ c. tomatoes, finely chopped

¼ c. green bell pepper, diced
⅛ - ¼ c. tarragon vinegar
2 green onions, finely chopped

Fill one half large or one small pocket bread in the following order: lettuce, green pepper, tomatoes seasoned with tarragon vinegar and pepper. Add 2-3 falafel patties and top with more shredded lettuce and chopped green onions.
Note: Heat patties in microwave and assemble at work, home or park. Serves 1.

Tomato-Yogurt Sauce

1 c. plain, low-fat yogurt
2 t. tomato puree
1 t. prepared horseradish

½ clove garlic, minced
1 t. parsley

Mix all ingredients. Cover and refrigerate.

MONDAY RECIPES

Breakfast

Bran Muffins

1 c. stone ground whole wheat flour	½ c. undiluted apple juice frozen concentrate
1 t. baking soda	¾ c. skim milk
1¾ c. bran	½ t. cinnamon
¼ c. fresh or frozen unsweetened blueberries	⅛ t. cloves, ground
	⅛ t. nutmeg
1 egg white	½ t. vanilla

Preheat oven to 400°. Mix together dry ingredients and blueberries. Add one egg white and milk. Stir only enough to blend. Pour mixture into non-stick muffin tins or spray cupcake tins with PAM. Bake at 400 degrees for 20-30 minutes. Makes 12.

Cran-Orange Drink

1 c. unsweetened cranberry juice	¼ c. lemon juice
1 quart fresh orange juice	1 qt. sparkling mineral water
2 c. unsweetened pineapple juice	1 slice lemon

Combine the juices and chill. Add mineral water, a slice of lemon and ice, if desired, just before serving. Makes 11.5 cups.

Lunch

Cukes in Yogurt

2 medium cucumbers, pared,
   seeded, and thinly sliced
2 cloves garlic
2 oz. green onions, chopped
1 c. plain yogurt

2 T. chopped fresh mint
¼ t. cumin
¼ t. ground pepper
½ t. lemon juice
4 tomato wedges

Place cucumbers in colander and let stand an hour. Rinse cucumbers in cold water and drain well. Crush garlic in small bowl. Add onions and remaining ingredients except lettuce. Serve immediately with tomato wedge garnish. Optional: Serve over lettuce.

Bean Sprout Coleslaw

2 small carrots grated
1 medium cucumber, peeled,
   seeded, and grated
1 T. chopped pimentos

2 c. fresh bean sprouts, cooked
2 green onions, cut into
   thin strips
Dressing (see recipe below)

Combine first four ingredients in a colander and drain all excess liquid. Place in bowl. Add onions and dressing. Serves 2.

Dressing

2 T. white vinegar
1 t. Worcestershire
1 t. paprika

2 t. celery seeds
2-3 T. fresh orange juice

Combine all ingredients in a jar, cover and chill.

Dinner

Mediterranean Meat Loaf

½ lb. lean ground beef/
   ½ lb. ground lamb
1 c. tomato sauce
3 egg whites
1½ t. ground cumin(or to taste)
½ c. barley
½ c. parsley, finely chopped

1 clove garlic, crushed
¼ t. oregano
¼ t. rosemary
¼ t. thyme
¼ t. basil
1 c. diced zucchini
¼ t. dry mustard

Combine all ingredients, shape into a loaf, place in a non-stick pan and bake 1 hour and 10 minutes at 350°. Serves 6.

Gazpacho

1 tomato, quartered
½ c. tomato juice
½ small garlic clove, crushed
2 T. finely chopped onion

1 t. vinegar
1 t. lemon juice
½ cucumber, chopped
1 green onion, finely chopped

Place the tomato, lemon juice, onion, garlic, vinegar and tomato juice into a blender and puree until smooth. Add half the cucumber and blend again. Serve chilled and top with remaining chopped cucumber and green onions. Serves 1.

Tabouli Salad

1 c. bulgar wheat
1 c. finely chopped parsley
½ c. finely chopped green onions
1 lb. tomatoes, coarsely chopped

1 c. chopped fresh mint
⅓ c. lemon juice
¼ t. fresh ground black pepper
romaine for garnish

Cover bulgar wheat with boiling water and let soak for 2 hours. Drain well. Add remaining ingredients and mix well. Let stand overnight in refrigerator. Serve on a bed of romaine. Serves 4-6.

Baked Apple

1 medium apple
cinnamon

1 t. seedless raisins

Core the apple and scrape off the skin from the top ½ inch. Sprinkle the cinnamon into the core of the cavity. Add the raisins. Place the apple in a small baking dish. Add water to cover the bottom ¼ of the apple. Bake in the oven at 350° for 30 minutes, or until the apple is tender. Serves 1.

TUESDAY RECIPES

Dinner

Broiled Herbed Chicken

½ lb. boneless chicken,
   skin and fat removed
2 T. undiluted orange juice
½ t. tarragon vinegar

1 t. oregano
¼ t. parsley flakes
1 t. basil
¼ t. dry mustard

Arrange the chicken in a broiler pan. In a bowl combine all ingredients and mix well. Brush half the mixture over the chicken. Broil for 6 minutes, or until the chicken is lightly browned. Turn and brush the other side with remaining herb mixture. Broil for 6 minutes more, or until chicken is tender. Serves 2.

Spiced Carrots

1½ c. carrots, sliced
½ c. water
¼ t. cinnamon

2 T. apple juice, frozen,
   unthawed
2 T. orange juice, frozen,
   unthawed

In a non-stick saucepan combine carrots and water. Cook covered over medium heat for 10 minutes. Add spices and juices. Cook an additional 10 minutes or until tender. Remove from heat. Drain and serve. Serves 2.

String Bean Salad

1 c. cooked, chopped
 string beans
1 c. cooked kidney
 beans, drained
1 medium onion, chopped

2 cloves garlic, minced
¼ c. vinegar
¼ c. water
1 T. lemon juice

Combine beans, onion and garlic. Cover with vinegar, water and lemon juice. Chill thoroughly. Serves 4.

Orange Fruit Cups

2 oranges
½ banana, sliced
1 apple, diced

4 t. raisins
4 T. plain, nonfat yogurt
1 T. cinnamon

Cut the oranges in half. With a grapefruit knife or spoon, remove the fruit from the rind, leaving the rind intact. Cut the orange segments into a bowl. Add the banana, apple, raisins, yogurt and cinnamon and mix well. Fill orange cups with this mixture. Chill and serve. Serves 4.

WEDNESDAY RECIPES

Breakfast

Strawberry Yogurt

2 c. sliced strawberries   2 c. nonfat yogurt

Stir strawberries into yogurt, crushing a few of the strawberry slices until yogurt turns pink. Refrigerate and serve. Serves 4.

Dinner

Veal Scallopini Marsala with Mushrooms

1 lb. veal, cut into ⅛   1 c. chicken bouillon
    to ¼ inch thick slices   ½ c. Marsala wine (or any
fresh ground pepper   sweet white wine)
½ t. cornstarch or arrowroot   1 T. fresh chopped parsley
½ clove garlic, crushed   1 t. lemon juice
2 c. sliced mushrooms

Pepper veal slices. Saute the mushrooms in 2 T. chicken stock and remove from non-stick saucepan. In the same pan, saute veal slices over high heat in 2 T. chicken stock for less than 20 seconds on each side. Veal should have a slightly pink tinge. Remove veal and keep with the mushrooms. To the same pan add Marsala, garlic, and remaining chicken stock. Simmer and add cornstarch (cornstarch should be dissolved in cold water first) stirring until dissolved. Add parsley and lemon juice. Pour this wine sauce over the veal and mushrooms and serve. Serves 4.

Wild Rice and Mushrooms

1 c. wild rice
3 T. each: finely minced carrots, onions, and celery
2 quarts boiling water
1 bay leaf
½ lb. fresh mushrooms, sliced
1 c. chicken broth or bouillon

2½-qt. fireproof casserole with cover
¼ t. thyme
¼ c. dry white wine
⅛ t. ground pepper

Preheat oven to 350°. Bring water to a boil and drop the rice in the boiling water. Boil uncovered for 5 minutes. Drain the rice. In a casserole dish saute the vegetables and mushrooms in white wine. Add to the rice the sauteed vegetables, beef bouillon, and remaining seasonings to taste. Boil for 1 minute. Cover the casserole and set in 350° preheated oven for 35 minutes or until rice is tender. Add a few drops more liquid if all liquid has been absorbed before rice is tender. Discard the bay leaf and serve. Serves 4.

Asparagus with Lemon-Parsley Sauce

1 bunch fresh asparagus
¼ c. lemon juice

2 T. fresh chopped parsley

Trim the bottom of the asparagus and wash well. Tie them loosely together in a bunch. Stand asparagus upright in 2 inches of water in a deep pot and cover. (In this way the tender tops steam as the bottoms boil). Cook until tender. Remove them from the water and arrange on a platter. Mix the lemon juice and parsley and pour over the asparagus and serve. Serves 4.

Herb Tomatoes Parmigiano

4 firm medium tomatoes,   2 T. oregano
   cut in half   2 T. basil
4 t. Parmesan cheese, grated
¼ t. ground pepper

Preheat oven to 400°. Arrange the tomatoes in a glass baking pan or non-stick pan. Add water enough to allow tomatoes to just barely sit in water – about ¼ inch. Sprinkle top of tomatoes with pepper, oregano, basil and cheese (½ t. to each tomato half). Bake in 400° oven for 20 minutes. Then place tomatoes under the broiler for 8 to 10 minutes, or until the tomato tops are slightly brown. Do not, however, overcook them, or they will lose their shape. Serves 4.

Sweet Potato Boat

1 sweet potato (5″ long x 2″) ⅛ t. ground nutmeg
2 T. orange juice   and/or cinnamon

Bake the sweet potato for 35 minutes, or until tender. Split the top open and scoop out the potato. Mash with the orange juice, cinnamon and nutmeg; refill the jacket. Eat warm or refrigerate and serve as a chilled dessert. Serves 1.

THURSDAY RECIPES

Breakfast

Marina del Egg

1 slice whole-wheat bread	1 egg white
toasted	dash of nutmeg
1 thin slice tomato	pepper, to taste

Cut out a circle in the center of the bread; place the bread in a non-stick skillet. Drop the egg white into the hole. Sprinkle with nutmeg. Cover and cook to desired doneness. Top with slice(s) of tomato.

Lunch

Tuna Salad

1 6-oz. can of water	¼ c. lemon juice
packed tuna	¼-½ small onion, diced finely
1 small head lettuce,	½ t. pepper
finely chopped	½ clove garlic, crushed
1 c. finely chopped celery	4 small tomatoes, cut in eighths
1 c. diced cucumber	4 green bell pepper rings
¼ c. vinegar	

Mix tuna, lettuce, celery and cucumber. In a separate bowl mix vinegar, lemon juice, onion, crushed garlic and pepper. Combine with tuna mixture. Garnish with tomato wedges and top with green pepper rings. Serves 4.

126

Dinner

Arroz Con Pollo (Rice with Chicken)

4 chicken legs with thigh,
    trimmed of skin and fat
¼ c. light wine vinegar
1 c. brown rice, cooked
1 c. sliced fresh mushrooms
½ c. finely chopped celery
1 c. chopped onion

2 cloves garlic, sliced
2½ c. chicken stock
1 28-oz. can whole tomatoes
¼ c. chopped pimento
6 T. chopped fresh parlsey
fresh ground pepper to taste
pinch of saffron

Poach chicken in white wine and water (4 cups).Remove chicken when just tender and place in a casserole dish. Reserve chicken broth. In a separate non-stick pan, combine cooked rice, mushrooms, onion, celery and garlic in ¼ c. poaching liquid and cook over moderate heat for 5 minutes. Add remaining poaching liquid, bring to a boil, cover and simmer for 20 minutes at a very low heat. Add remaining ingredients, heat to boiling and pour over chicken in casserole. Cover and bake at 350° F. for 45 minutes. Remove cover and cook 10 minutes more. Serves 4.

Zucchini Espanola

2 medium zucchini,
    sliced ¼" thick
1 1-lb. can tomatoes,
    finely chopped
1 medium onion, diced

½ c. fresh parsley, finely
    chopped
1 T. dried parsley flakes
¼ t. ground thyme
⅛ t. ground pepper

Place the zucchini, tomatoes and onion in a non-stick saucepan. Add ¼ cup parsley, thyme and pepper. Cook, covered, over medium flame for 10-15 minutes until the zucchini is tender. Sprinkle remaining ¼ cup fresh parsley just before serving. Serves 4.

FRIDAY RECIPES

Breakfast

Egg Omelet

¼ fresh onion,
    finely chopped
¼ c. evaporated skim milk
2 egg whites, beaten to
    fluffy peaks

¼ c. canned mushrooms, drained
    and sliced – or freshly sliced
    mushrooms
pepper to taste

In a small bowl combine onion and milk. Let stand for 5-10 minutes. Fold in egg white and remaining ingredients. Pour into a non-stick skillet. Cook over low heat, stirring until egg is set. Serves 1.

Apple Shake

Blend ½ c. skim milk, ¼ t. vanilla and 1 chopped apple. Serve topped with nutmeg and cinnamon.

Lunch

Spinach and Mushroom Salad

1 lb. fresh spinach   **1 hard boiled egg white**
¼ lb. fresh mushrooms

Trim and wash the spinach carefully and place in a salad bowl. Wash and slice the mushrooms; add them to the spinach. Discard the yolk of the egg, and chop the egg white; add it to the spinach. Add 2 tablespoons of the BHMD salad dressing of your choice. Toss and serve. Serves 4.

Fresh Garden Soup

½ c. diced potato
1⅓ c. chopped onions
1¾ c. chopped celery
¾ c. chopped carrots
1¾ c. chopped rutabagas
¾ c. chopped zucchini
¾ c. sliced mushrooms
¾ c. shredded cabbage
¾ c. cauliflower
8 c. water

¾ c. canned diced tomatoes or fresh
¾ c. canned tomato puree or fresh
¾ t. Italian seasoning if desired
1 garlic clove, crushed or minced finely
1-2 bay leaves
1 t. each oregano, basil (or to taste)

Bring the water and tomato ingredients to a boil. Add all the vegetables and seasonings. Reduce the heat, cooking until the vegetables are done. May be refrigerated for 2-3 weeks.

Dinner

Steak

1 - 4 oz. top round sirloin   **dash of pepper**
¼ c. red burgundy wine

Marinate beef in wine for 15 minutes, turning occasionally. Broil to desired doneness.

Brown Rice

1 c. brown rice   **2 c. water, if using long-grain rice, or 1¾ c. water if using short-grain rice**

Bring water to a boil. Add rice and return to boil. Lower flame to simmer, cover pot and cook for 35-40 minutes. Serves 3-4.

Stuffed Zucchini

4 8-inch zucchini
½ c. matzo meal
¼ c. minced fresh parsley
2 T. grated Parmesan cheese
¾ c. skinned and diced
    fresh tomato

½ c. finely chopped onion
¼ c. finely chopped green pepper
1 c. cooked brown rice
½ garlic clove, crushed

Slice the zucchini in half lengthwise. Scrape out the pulp from the centers. Place the zucchini shells in a pan in a little boiling water and simmer for a few minutes until partially cooked (keeping firm enough for stuffing). Set aside. Mix zucchini pulp with the other ingredients in a bowl. Stuff zucchini and place in casserole dish. Cover and bake in preheated oven (350°) for 45 minutes. Uncover and brown for 10-15 minutes. Serve plain or with spaghetti sauce (see Sauces, Chapter Seventeen). Serves 4.

SATURDAY RECIPES

Breakfast

Tomato Cocktail

1 c. (uncreamed 99.5% fat-free) cottage cheese

3 c. chilled tomato juice

½ garlic clove, crushed

2 T. finely chopped onion

4 T. finely chopped celery

In a blender mix all ingredients thoroughly and serve. Makes 4 cups.

Potato Pancakes

2 medium potatoes, cooked and peeled

4 egg whites

½ c. yogurt

¼ c. grated onion

2 T. fresh parsley, finely chopped

1 T. whole wheat flour

pepper to taste

Grate potatoes into egg whites. Add remaining ingredients and stir well. Drop mixture on hot Teflon skillet forming pancakes. Brown on both sides and serve with yogurt and/or applesauce. Makes 16 small pancakes.

Lunch

Vegetable Cream Soup

½ c. cooked vegetables
(asparagus, broccoli,
peas, etc.)
½ c. skim milk

dash of pepper
herbs (thyme, marjoram,
rosemary, etc.) to taste

Put all ingredients into an electric blender and process until smooth. Heat and serve. Serves 1. Note: Use left-over cooked vegetables to whip up instant and delicious soups.

Dinner

Curried Beef

½ lb. leanest ground beef
4 T. curry powder
½ red apple with skin, chopped
1 small onion, chopped
¼ green bell pepper, chopped
3 celery stalks, chopped
1 large carrot, grated
   or shredded

½ c. zucchini, finely diced
4 T. raisins
juice of 1 fresh orange
freshly ground pepper
1 c. water

Cook beef in non-stick skillet until nearly brown. Add all the vegetables, curry and orange juice. Mix well. Add water. If you like a hotter curry, add more. You may add more water to get a sauce at the bottom of the pan. Simmer for 15 minutes. Place ¼ of the curry over ½ c. of steaming brown rice. Note: to make things go easier, make your steamed brown rice first while you are cooking the curried burger. Serves 4.

Steamed Eggplant

1 medium eggplant or ½ lb.   **¼ t. ground pepper**
¼ c. lemon juice

Peel the eggplant and cut it in half lengthwise. (See Eggplant Hints). Brush each piece with lemon juice and fresh ground pepper. Place in a steamer. (see Steaming Hints) over boiling water and cover tightly. Steam for 15-20 minutes, or until tender. Optional: Serve with Spaghetti sauce. (See Sauces, Chapter Seventeen).   Serves 2.

Frozen Banana

Peel firm ripe banana, insert popsicle stick into end of banana. Place in a small plastic bag. Put in freezer. Serve as dessert or as fresh fruit popsicle on those hot days when ice cream is desired.

Brunch

Oven-Fried Potatoes

The easiest method is to start with baked potatoes. Once baked potatoes cool, slice lengthwise as French fries or into round slice "cottage style" fries. Spread the potatoes out on a non-stick baking sheet and season with curry, paprika, or chili powder. "Fry" in a 350° oven, turning "fries" with a spatula to brown both sides. "Fry" until crispy. Note: Bake several potatoes to keep in the refrigerator for snacks, especially oven-fried potatoes.

Cheese-Zucchini Quiche

1 c. (uncreamed 99.5% fat-free) cottage cheese
1 c. skim milk
½ c. diced onions
½ c. zucchini, finely diced
3 green onions, finely diced
1 t. prepared hot mustard
¼ t. fresh garlic juice
2 T. chopped pimento
dash nutmeg
1 T. vermouth

Put all ingredients except pimento into blender and blend at high speed until mixture becomes creamy. Pour into a 8-inch Teflon pie pan, and bake at 325° F. Garnish with pimento and continue baking until nicely browned (about 30 minutes). Serves 4.

Tomato Salad

1 sliced tomato
pinch of oregano and basil

tarragon vinegar
fresh ground pepper

Thinly slice tomato, layer on plate, and top with vinegar and seasonings.
Serves 1.

Mandarin Pudding

1 envelope unflavored gelatin
2 c. water, divided
⅔ c. skim milk

4 T. frozen undiluted apple juice
1 T. almond extract (or to taste)
1 large, very ripe banana

Sprinkle gelatin over ½ c. water in small non-stick saucepan. Heat, stirring
until gelatin dissolves. Pour into blender. Add remaining water, skim milk,
apple juice, banana and almond extract; blend thoroughly in blender. Pour
into four ½ cup molds or parfait glasses. Chill. Makes 4 servings.

Dinner

Baked Brown Rice with Mushrooms

4 T. water
½ c. finely chopped onion
1 t. finely minced garlic
1 c. brown rice

1½ c. unsalted chicken broth
¼ lb. mushrooms, freshly sliced
1 bay leaf

Preheat oven to 400°. Heat water in non-stick saucepan and add the onion, mushrooms and garlic. Stir until onion wilts. Bring water to a boil in a casserole dish and add the rice and stir (add a bit more water if necessary). Add the chicken broth and bay leaf and return to a boil. Cover saucepan and place in oven. Bake the rice for 45 minutes. Serves 4.

Tandoori Chicken

1-4 oz. boneless chicken breast,
skin and fat removed
3 T. plain yogurt
½ clove garlic, crushed/minced
¼ t. black pepper
pinch ground red hot pepper
1 T. white vinegar

1 t. minced papaya (optional)
½ t. ground ginger
⅓ t. ground coriander
⅓ t. ground cumin seed
1 T. lime juice
Thin lemon slices
Coriander leaves

With a sharp knife cut several slits on the breast. Mix all the other ingredients except lemon slices and coriander leaves. Marinate the chicken in this mixture for 6 or 7 hours or overnight in the refrigerator. Place breast under broiler and broil for 6 minutes or until chicken is lightly browned. Turn and broil for 6 more minutes or until chicken is tender. Serve hot, garnished with thin lemon slices and coriander leaves. Serves 1.

Glazed Yams

3 large yams, pared and sliced ⅛ t. Angostura Bitters
3 c. water 4 T. raisins
2 c. orange juice 2 t. cornstarch or arrowroot

Combine all ingredients except cornstarch in a non-stick saucepan. Cook over medium heat until yams are tender. In a separate pan mix the cornstarch with the cooking liquid and cook until thickened. Pour thickened liquid over yams and serve. Serves 4.

CHAPTER SIXTEEN:

EVERYDAY: MODERATE WEIGHT LOSS

FREEDOM WITH RESPONSIBILITY

You come to this chapter either after having surfaced from the Plunge or because you wish to lose weight in a more moderate fashion. On the Everyday approach you continue to slim but less dramatically than on the Plunge. If you stick to this broader version of the Plunge your weight loss will average between five and ten pounds a month.

From a quick look at the Everday menus you'll notice that the selection permits considerably more freedom than that of the Plunge. But this freedom entails responsibility.

The key to the Everyday weight-loss chart is calorie-counting. You are permitted to mix different recipes and to redesign the menus according to your personal preferences – *provided you don't exceed the 1,200-calorie limit*. In constructing your own menus, consult the BHMD calorie chart to determine the calorie count of each recipe. Unlike the Plunge, where you must not mix and combine different recipes, the Everyday program calls on self-restraint to keep your appetite within the prescribed bounds.

Fortunately, the Everyday recipes are so designed as to assist your sense of responsibility. They do so by minimizing temptations. The fact that you're allowed more calories and a wider variety of recipes is already a strong deterrent to overeating. But a far greater restraint is excercised by the fact that within a week or two – if not days – you'll be turning up your nose at the fattening fare of yore.

Once you've really gotten into the BHMD the things of old just won't taste so good any more. That's the long and short of the diet's effectiveness. Your tastes for sweets especially take a dive. You'll find that rich and creamy desserts, for instance, no longer seem irresistible. Where before you might have consumed oodles of salt, you'll find soon after starting the BHMD that only a few grains suffice. Learn to dilute your animal protein with vegetables and grains. And so it goes, till you actually prefer the slim way of eating on the BHMD's Thin Cuisine.

If you come to the Everyday Weight Loss after the Plunge you will already be familiar with the many cooking techniques implicit in the recipes. On the Everyday plan these methods will become permanently fixed in your gastronomic repertoire.

I've said all along that on the BHMD you eat all the time. Here then is the way to do it:

STUFF FOR THE BAGGIE:
EAT ALL YOU WANT *

Raw vegetables for salads and snacks

cabbage	cress, garden	peppers, green
cauliflower	cucumber	radish
carrots	endive	romaine
celery	escarole	tomatoes
chicory	lettuce	watercress

Please note: if you choose vegetables for cooking from the low calorie groups I and II below, you can have ½ cup portions of 4 vegetables from group I and ½ cup portions of 2 vegetables from group II for an average of only 100 calories.

140

GROUP I (extremely low in calories)

asparagus	cauliflower	mushrooms
bean sprouts	celery	mustard greens
beans, string	chard	rhubarb
beet, greens	chives	spinach
broccoli	collards	squash, summer
cabbage	dandelion, greens	turnip, greens

GROUP II (very low in calories)

bamboo shoots	fennel	scallions (6)
beets	kohlrabi	tomatoes
Brussels sprouts	leeks	tomato, juice
carrots	okra	turnips
eggplant	rutabagas	

*See Sauces, Chapter Seventeen. For a change of pace, take a plastic container with one of the BHMD's delectable dips or salad dressings in combination with raw vegetables. Suggested serving size ½ cup.

14-DAY EVERYDAY
WEIGHT LOSS PROGRAM

The following menus are constructed for 1,200 calories a day.

Breakfast
>Tomato Juice
>Marina del Egg
>"Sausage"

1

Lunch
>Bean Tostada
>1 orange or apple

Dinner
>Lettuce and Tomato Salad*
>Spanish Brown Rice
>Chiles Rellenos
>2 steamed corn tortillas
>Brown Rice Pudding

Breakfast
>Marina del Egg
>Tomato Juice
>"Sausage"
>½ grapefruit

2

Lunch
>Peach Puffs
>Garbanzos in Pita Bread
>Vegetable Cream Soup

Dinner
>Salad with WIN-VIN Dressing
>Fresh Garden Soup
>Veal Stuffed Peppers
>steamed broccoli
>Everyday Cheesecake with Strawberries

Breakfast
Quick Breakfast Drink
or
Banana Shake

Lunch
Tuna with Caper Sauce
or
3   Tangy Tuna
4 Finn or Ry-Krisp Crackers

Dinner
Lettuce and Tomato Salad
Shrimp Stuffed Trout
Yogurt Scalloped Potatoes
Artichokes in White Sauce
Orange Fruit Cup

*See Salad Dressings, Chapter Seventeen. As with all lettuce and tomato choices, use a couple of tablespoons of the dressings provided or use the same basic ingredients and create your own low-fat, low-salt recipes.

Breakfast
>   Oatmeal with Stewed Apples
>   Quick Breakfast Drink

Lunch
>   Tangy Tuna
>   4 Finn or Ry-Krisp crackers
>   2 pieces of fruit

4

Dinner
>   Lettuce and Tomato Salad
>   Baked Cod
>   ½ c. Black Beans
>   ½ c. brown rice
>   Fruit Salad Trieste

Breakfast
>   ½ grapefruit
>   French Toast

Lunch
>   Italian Vegetable Soup
>   4 Kavli or Finn crackers
>   pear or apple

5

Dinner
>   Italian Green Beans and Tomatoes
>   Asparagus Quiche
>   Pickled Cauliflower
>   Veal Scallopini
>   Baked potato
>   Apple Spice Cake

Breakfast
> Marina del Egg
> Quick Breakfast Drink

Lunch

6
> Bean Tostada
> Italian Vegetable Soup
> 4 Finn or Kavli crackers
> 1 piece fruit

Dinner
> Lettuce and Tomato Salad
> 4 oz. broiled steak
> Eggplant over Pasta
> steamed spinach
> Orange Sherbet

Breakfast
> Bran Muffin
> Quick Breakfast Drink

Lunch

7
> Athenian Salad
> Italian Vegetable Soup
> 4 Kavli or Finn crackers
> or
> 1 slice garlic toast*
> 1 piece fruit

Dinner
> Lettuce and Tomato Salad
> baked potato
> 2 broiled baby lamb chops (4 oz.)
> Glazed Carrots
> Peach Melba

*See Garlic in Hint Chapter for low-cal technique.

NOTE: For breakfast choose any from the foregoing Everyday breakfast programs.

8

Lunch
> Chicken Curry Salad Pocket Sandwich
> apple

Dinner
> Minestrone Soup
> Lettuce and Tomato Salad
> Italian Stuffed Green Peppers
> Slice of garlic toast
> Blueberry Melba

9

Lunch
> Cold Lentil Salad
> Bean Sprout Salad (see Plunge)
> 1 slice garlic toast

Dinner
> Sweet & Sour Bean Salad
> 2 Ratatouille Crepes (see Plunge for
> Ratatouille recipe)
> 4-oz. small baby lamb chops. broiled
> 1 slice garlic toast
> Orange Cup

10

Lunch
> Falafel Sandwich (see Plunge)
> 1 apple

Dinner
> Lettuce and Tomato Salad
> Mexican Beef Stew
> Spanish Brown Rice
> Pinto Beans
> Banana Flambe

Lunch
Italian Vegetable Soup
Potato Salad Sandwich

11   1 apple

Dinner
Lettuce and Tomato Salad
Broiled Fish with Lime Sauce
Empress Vegetables
Brown Rice Parmigiana
Apple-Spice Cake

Lunch
Health Sandwich
1 apple

12

Dinner
Lettuce and Tomato Salad
Shish Kebob
steamed vegetable (broccoli,
    cauliflower, etc.)
Curry Rice
garlic toast
Orange Cup

13

Lunch
Tuna Salad Sandwich
Onion Soup
apple and orange

Dinner
Lettuce and Tomato Salad
Minestrone Soup
1 3-oz. broiled baby lamb chop
Zucchini and Pasta
Herbed Carrots
Fresh Fruit (apple, banana, orange)

14

Lunch
Lettuce and Tomato Salad
Pocket Pizza
apple or orange

Dinner
Lettuce and Tomato Salad
Garlic Soup
Sweet Cabbage Rolls
Baked Potato
Camden Drive Quiche

Breakfast

"Sausage"

1 c. ground chicken breast	½ garlic clove, crushed
1 egg white	1 T. bran
1 c. ground veal	⅛ t. sage
¼ c. cold water	½ t. rosemary
¼ t. fresh ground pepper	

Combine all ingredients thoroughly. Shape into patties and store in freezer. This quantity yields 16 patties at 25 calories each. To cook, fry patties at low heat in covered Teflon pan until done. Note: For Italian sausage simply double the amount of garlic and add anise to taste. For a spicier fare, add ½ t. ground red chile pepper. Serving: 3 sausages.

Lunch

Bean Tostada

2-6 inch corn tortillas	2 T. green onions, finely chopped
4 oz. cooked pinto beans	1 medium tomato, chopped
2 T. Jack cheese, grated	2 T. cilantro, finely chopped
4 T. red chile sauce*	(optional)
1 T. green chile, chopped	1 c. shredded lettuce

Heat tortillas over gas burner on stove or under broiler until toasted on each side. Mash beans in some of its own liquid or water. Spread tortillas with the beans and top with cheese. Heap on the tomatoes and lettuce. Top with chile sauce, green onions and cilantro. Serves 1.

*See Sauces, Chapter Seventeen.

Dinner

Spanish Brown Rice

1¾ c. water
1 c. brown rice
½ c. green pepper,
    finely chopped
½ c. onions, finely chopped

4 oz. tomato paste
½ t. chili powder
¼ t. cumin
1 t. freshly ground pepper
    (optional)

Bring water to a rolling boil and add rice, stirring well. Add the remaining ingredients and stir. When rice returns to a boil reduce heat, cover and simmer for 50 minutes. Let cool 20 minutes and serve. Serves 4.

Sauce for Chiles Rellenos

1 lb. fresh tomatoes
2 T. onion, chopped
1 T. fresh orange juice
½ small clove garlic, crushed
pinch of cinnamon, or 1 whole
    cinnamon stick

5 whole cloves
8 whole peppercorns
1 small bay leaf
dash nutmeg (optional)

Before preparing Chiles Rellenos, parboil tomatoes 30-60 seconds. Remove skin and seeds and place tomatoes in blender. Place the next four ingredients in blender and puree. Bring to a low boil in saucepan. Add remaining ingredients and simmer for 5-10 minutes. Serve over rellenos.

Chiles Rellenos in Sauce

4 green chiles
    (remove seeds and wash)
4 egg whites

1 c. hoop cheese
pinch of salt and cream of tartar

Beat egg white with salt and cream of tartar until stiff peaks form. Stuff each chile with ¼ c. hoop cheese. Pat stuffed chile with paper towel to dry. Sprinkle with slight amount of whole wheat flour to cover completely. Spread half of the egg batter on a non-stick baking sheet in an area about the size of the 4 chiles. Place chiles on top, then cover with remaining egg white batter. Bake at 350° for 15 minutes. Top with sauce and serve. Serves 2.

Brown Rice Pudding

1 c. brown rice
1½ c. water
2 c. skim milk
2 T. dry nonfat milk
2 egg whites, slightly beaten

¼ c. raisins
½ t. vanilla
8 T. apple juice
Cinnamon and nutmeg to taste
1 cinnamon stick (optional)

Preheat oven to 300°. Bring rice and 1 cup water to a boil in a fireproof casserole dish. Cover and simmer 25 minutes. Mix the remaining ingredients together except cinnamon, nutmeg and cinnamon stick, and add to the cooked rice, stirring thoroughly. Sprinkle with nutmeg, cinnamon and stir. Add cinnamon stick. Bake uncovered in 300° oven for 1 hour and 15 minutes. Spoon 2 T. apple juice over each serving to sweeten. Optional: 2 T. skim milk over each serving if a moister pudding is desired. Serves 4.

Lunch

Peach Puffs

12 peach halves, water packed ¼ t. frozen apple juice
whole cloves   concentrate
1 c. hoop cheese   ¼ t. lemon juice

Insert 2 cloves into each peach half and chill an hour. Mix hoop cheese, apple juice concentrate and lemon juice in a blender. Fill the remaining six peach halves with the mixture and put the other halves on top of the stuffed peaches, forming whole peaches. Chill. Remove cloves before serving. Serves 6.

Garbanzos in Pita Bread

½ whole wheat pita bread   ½ small tomato, diced
½ c. cooked garbanzo beans ¼ t. garlic powder
2 T. chives   1 T. tarragon vinegar
½ c. shredded lettuce

Combine the garbanzo beans, onions, lettuce, tomato and garlic powder and mix with the tarragon vinegar. Stuff this mixture into the pita bread. Note: a small amount of water packed tuna may be added, if desired. Serves 1.

Veal Stuffed Peppers

2 green peppers,
    halved and seeded
8 oz. boneless veal shoulder,
    cut into 1" cubes
½ t. pepper
1 t. oregano

1 clove garlic, crushed
½ small onion, finely diced
2 T. fresh parsley
½ c. chicken bouillon
¼ c. lemon juice
2 T. tomato juice

Dip peppers in boiling water for 2 minutes and drain. Brown veal in a non-stick pan over moderate heat with pepper, oregano and garlic. Stuff veal into pepper halves and set in baking dish. Combine onion, parsley, bouillon, lemon juice, tomato juice and water and bring to a boil. Pour this mixture evenly into each pepper half. Bake at 325° for 20-30 minutes. Serves 2.

Everyday Cheesecake with Strawberries

3½ c. hoop cheese
1 c. nonfat buttermilk
2 envelopes unflavored gelatin
1 small can unsweetened
    crushed pineapple

½ c. undiluted frozen apple
    juice concentrate, thawed
½ c. water
1 t. vanilla extract
3 egg whites
1½ c. Grape Nuts cereal

Break up hoop cheese by hand. Add enough to fill blender half full. Add ½ c. buttermilk and blend until thick and smooth. Remove cheese mixture to a bowl and repeat procedure with remaining cheese and buttermilk. Pour in with the rest of cheese mixture. In another bowl mix the gelatin with the pineapple thoroughly. In a pan combine apple juice and water and bring to a boil. Pour this boiling liquid in with gelatin mixture and stir until dissolved. Let cool. Meanwhile, beat egg whites until stiff peaks form. Now thoroughly mix gelatin with cheese mixture and vanilla. Fold egg whites into the cheese batter completely. For instant crust, moisten the Grape Nuts cereal with a little apple juice. Spread evenly across the bottom of a 9-inch pie pan to form the bottom crust. Pour the cheese batter into the pan and chill. Cover with fruit topping and serve.

Fruit Topping

1 bag frozen strawberries, or
    unsweetened blueberries
¼ c. undiluted frozen apple
    juice concentrate, thawed

¼ c. water
1 t. vanilla extract
1-2 t. cornstarch or arrowroot

Bring frozen strawberries or blueberries to a boil in the apple juice and water. Thicken with cornstarch which has been blended first with a little cold water. Stir in vanilla and cool. Spread over the pie and refrigerate until the topping has set.

Breakfast

Banana Shake

1 very ripe banana
¼ tsp. vanilla
1 c. skim milk

1 T. regular nonfat dry milk
1 T. cinnamon
3 ice cubes

Slice the banana, combine all ingredients in a blender, and mix until ice is crushed. Makes 1 shake.

Lunch

Tuna with Caper Sauce

1 6-oz. can water packed tuna **½ tomato, sliced**
romaine lettuce leaves **1 lemon wedge**
Caper Sauce

Pour desired amount of Caper Sauce over the tuna and mix. Serve on a bed of lettuce and garnish with tomato slices on the side. Use lemon to taste. Serves

Caper Sauce

4 c. thinly sliced celery **½ c. capers**
4 c. beef bouillon **¼ c. caper liquid**

In a large saucepan cook celery and bouillon until celery becomes soft. Place in a blender and process until smooth. Return to saucepan. Stir in remaining ingredients. Simmer until thickened. Makes 8 servings.

Dinner

Shrimp Stuffed Trout

2 shallots, chopped
4 mushrooms, finely chopped
1 garlic clove, crushed
¼ c. dry sherry
½ c. chicken stock
4 raw shrimp, finely chopped

2 T. whole wheat bread crumbs
2 T. chopped parsley
pepper to taste
5-oz. boneless trout
paprika to taste

Saute the shallots, mushrooms and garlic in 1 tablespoon of the chicken stock. Add sherry, stock and shrimp and simmer until enough liquid evaporates to leave a thick mixture. Add 1 tablespoon bread crumbs and 1 tablespoon parsley. Season with pepper to taste. Divide the mixture into four equal parts and stuff the cavity of each fish. Sprinkle with remaining bread crumbs and parsley. Wrap fish in aluminum foil and set on a non-stick baking pan. Bake in 400° F. oven for 25 minutes or until done. After the first 10 minutes of baking, open the foil and baste fish in its own juices every five minutes to prevent dryness. Serves 1.

Yogurt Scalloped Potatoes

6 new potatoes, washed and
   sliced (not peeled)
3 c. yogurt
1½ c. cottage cheese
   (uncreamed)

3 T. Parmesan cheese, grated
½ c. beef stock
¾ c. fresh chopped parsley
¾ c. sliced green onions

Cover potatoes with boiling water, boil until just tender, and drain. Blend yogurt and cottage cheese in blender until very smooth. Combine stock, parsley and green onions in a pan and simmer until onions soften. Add yogurt and cheese blend to make sauce. Arrange potato slices in a shallow casserole dish, top with 3 tablespoons Parmesan, pour sauce over top and bake 30 minutes at 350°. Set under broiler close to flame for 2 minutes before serving. Serves 4.

Artichokes in White Sauce

16 oz. cooked artichoke hearts
   or 16 oz. canned packed
   in water
¼ c. buttermilk

1 T. dry white wine
⅛ t. marjoram leaves
½ garlic clove, crushed

Combine all ingredients in a saucepan. Cook over low heat for 5 minutes. Makes 2 servings.

Breakfast

Oatmeal with Stewed Apples

2 c. rolled oats   ½ t. vanilla
2 c. boiling water   ¼ t. ground cinnamon
1 apple, thinly sliced   Skim milk

Stir the oats into the boiling water. Cook and stir for several minutes. Add the remaining ingredients and cook 10 minutes, stirring occasionally. Serve hot with warm skim milk. Serves 4.

Dinner

Baked Cod

1 lb. cod filets   ¼ t. pepper

Bake at 375° for 10 minutes, until fish flakes easily with a fork. Just before removing from oven coat with Mustard Cream Sauce (see Sauces, p. 185). Serves 3.

Black Beans

1 c. black beans
2 c. water
1 whole garlic clove

1 bay leaf
1 t. fresh ground pepper

Soak beans overnight in plenty of water. Or, to quick soak, boil the beans for 2-5 minutes, cover and remove from stove. Let sit 1 hour. Discard soaking water before cooking. Bring 2 cups water to a boil and add all of the ingredients. Reduce heat to a simmer and cook 45 minutes or until completely tender. Discard bay leaf and whole garlic. Serves 4.

Fruit Salad Trieste

1 fresh apple, diced
16-oz. pineapple chunks,
    fresh or water packed
1 orange, diced

4 T. fresh orange juice
2 egg whites
⅛ t. cream of tartar
½ t. almond extract
½ t. vanilla extract

Mix apple, pineapple, orange and orange juice. Scoop the fruit into 4 individual oven-proof pudding dishes. Beat the egg whites until soft peaks form. Add cream of tartar and continue beating until stiff peaks form. Add the almond extract and vanilla. Heap the creamy whites on top of the fruit salad, spreading it to the edges of the dishes. Place in a preheated 400° oven for 5-7 minutes, or until a brown meringue forms. Serves 4.

Breakfast

French Toast

1 egg white	½ t. vanilla extract
¼ c. skim milk	2 slices whole wheat bread
¼ t. cinnamon	½ c. applesauce, unsweetened

Beat together vigorously the egg white, milk, cinnamon and vanilla. Dip the bread slices into this batter. Cook the bread in a non-stick skillet, turning when browned on one side. When both sides are brown, serve with applesauce. Serves 1.

Lunch

Italian Vegetable Soup

1¼ c. chopped onions	2 28-oz. cans tomatoes, diced
½ c. chopped celery	½ 15-oz. can tomato paste
½ c. carrots, sliced	4 c. water
1 c. cooked kidney beans	2 bay leaves
1¾ c. chopped turnips	1 t. dried parsley
2 c. chopped zucchini	1 t. basil
½ c. sliced green beans	1 clove garlic, crushed

Blend the water, tomatoes and tomato paste together. Bring to a low boil. Add all the vegetables except zucchini. Return to boil, reduce heat and simmer until vegetables are half-done. Add the zucchini and seasonings and continue cooking until all vegetables are tender. Top each bowl with a pinch of grated Parmesan cheese. Makes 16 servings.

Dinner

Italian Green Beans and Tomatoes

1 lb. fresh green beans,
   trimmed and sliced
2 fresh tomatoes, finely chopped
½ t. basil

½ t. dried oregano
1 t. fresh parsley
⅛ t. ground pepper
1 c. water

Combine all ingredients in a non-stick pan and cook until the beans are tender and crisp, about 15-20 minutes. Drain and serve. Serves 4.

Asparagus Quiche

8 oz. fresh asparagus, chopped
1 T. green onions,
   finely chopped
1 T. green pepper, chopped
1 T. beef bouillon

4 egg whites
2 T. cottage cheese, uncreamed
2 t. skim milk
1 t. parsley, chopped
ground pepper to taste

Boil the asparagus until very tender. Chop the asparagus into small bits and place in a small non-stick skillet. Add the green onion and green pepper and saute over low heat in 1 tablespoon beef bouillon until the vegetables are tender. Beat the egg whites until soft peaks form. Mix egg whites, cheese, skim milk, parsley and pepper until smooth. Pour the batter over the vegetables in the skillet and mix. Cook over low flame until the bottom browns. Loosen the edges with a spatula and turn over to brown on the other side. Place in a 300° F. oven for 15 minutes. Serves 2.

Pickled Cauliflower

1 lb. cauliflower
¼ c. white wine
½ c. tarragon vinegar
1 t. peppercorns, ground

1 T. green chile pepper, chopped
⅛ t. paprika
1 t. dill seed
½ clove garlic, sliced

Cook flowerets in ½ c. boiling water for 10-15 minutes. Combine the remaining ingredients with cooking liquid to make the marinade. Marinate the cauliflower 24 hours in the refrigerator. Makes 3-4 servings.

Veal Scallopini

1 c. bouillon
1 lb. veal, cut up
1 clove garlic, finely minced
1 c. canned mushrooms, or ½
    lb. freshly sliced

1 small bay leaf
½ t. basil
½ t. oregano
1 T. tomato sauce

Heat ¼ cup bouillon in a non-stick pan and add veal. Brown on both sides. Add remaining bouillon, garlic, mushrooms, tomato sauce and bay leaf. Cover and cook over low heat until veal is tender to the touch. During the last few minutes of cooking, season with pepper, oregano and basil. Serves 4.

Apple Spice Cake

4 c. apples (6), finely chopped
½ c. undiluted apple juice, unsweetened frozen
½ c. water
¼ c. raisins
1¼ c. whole wheat pastry flour
1¼ c. rice flour (available in food stores)
2 t. each of baking powder and baking soda
2 T. cinnamon
⅛ t. nutmeg
⅛ t. allspice (optional)
4 egg whites
2 t. vanilla
1 c. Grape Nuts cereal

Preheat oven to 325 degrees. Combine first four ingredients in bowl. Cover and refrigerate for 1-2 hours. Meanwhile sift the remaining dry ingredients into a large bowl. In a separate bowl, beat the egg whites until soft peaks form. Then fold into the flour mixture. Add vanilla, cereal and apple mixture. Stirring thoroughly. Pour into a non-stick cake pan. Bake for 1½ hours at 325 degrees. When done turn cake out onto aluminum foil. Wrap cake tightly with foil. Let cool, then refrigerate for several hours or overnight. Keep stored in refrigerator.

Serves 12.

Dinner

Eggplant over Pasta

8 oz. whole wheat spaghetti
1 medium eggplant (1 lb.),
    sliced into ½″ sections
2 medium tomatoes, peeled
    and thinly sliced
4 oz. onions, thinly sliced

1 medium green pepper, cut
    into thin strips
½ t. garlic powder
oregano, crushed, to taste
sweet basil, crushed, to taste
pepper to taste
8 oz. hoop cheese
4 T. Parmesan cheese, grated

First, rub eggplant with garlic powder. In a casserole alternate layers of eggplant, tomato, onions, green pepper, spices, seasonings and cheese (sprinkle Parmesan cheese over the hoop cheese on each layer). Repeat layers, ending with cheese. Cover and bake at 350° F. for 20 minutes; uncover, and continue to bake another 30 minutes until eggplant is done. Serve the baked Eggplant Casserole over cooked pasta. Serves 4.

Orange Sherbet

1 6-oz. can frozen orange
    juice concentrate
1½ c. skim milk

⅔ c. nonfat dry milk
3 drops vanilla

Combine all ingredients in blender and blend until mixed. Place in freezer until firm. Serving size: 1 cup.

Lunch

Athenian Salad

2 c. spinach (raw)
¼ c. brown rice, cooked
1 small sweet red pimento,
   cut into ¼" strips
1 small cucumber, diced

1½ oz. crumbled feta cheese
2 T. WIN-VIN Dressing
1 slice garlic toast

Mix spinach with rice, pimento, cucumber, and feta cheese. Add dressing and mix lightly. Cut the garlic toast into cubes to make croutons and top off salad. Serves 1.

Dinner

Glazed Carrots

8 large carrots, thinly sliced
¼ c. undiluted frozen apple
   juice, thawed
1 T. grated orange rind

1 t. cornstarch or arrowroot
⅛ t. ground ginger

Steam or boil the carrots until tender. Mix the apple juice, orange rind, cornstarch or arrowroot and ginger in a saucepan until smooth. Cook over low flame, stirring constantly, until the glaze thickens and clears. Add the cooked carrots and coat all sides with the glaze. Serve hot. Serves 4.

Peach Melba

1 pint lowfat yogurt	1 T. undiluted frozen apple juice
1 t. vanilla extract	concentrate, thawed
1 c. red raspberries,	6 canned peach halves, water
frozen without sugar	packed, drained

Mix the yogurt and vanilla. Puree the raspberries in blender. Add ¼ cup puree to the yogurt and mix well. Place this mixture in freezer for several hours. Mix the remaining puree and apple juice in a blender. Set this sauce aside. Set each peach half in a pudding dish and chill in refrigerator until ready to serve. Top each peach half with a scoop of frozen yogurt. Spoon on the raspberry sauce and serve.

Serves 6.

Lunch

Chicken Curry Salad Pocket Sandwich

1 large slice of pineapple, diced	2 T. low-fat yogurt
1 t. curry powder	2 oz. water chestnuts, diced
⅛ t. dry mustard	¼ c. diced celery
2 oz. cooked chicken, shredded	¼ clove garlic, crushed
¼ medium green pepper, diced	

In a bowl combine curry, yogurt, garlic, mustard and pineapple. Mix thoroughly and stir in the remaining ingredients. Stuff a whole pita bread with shredded lettuce and tomato. Add the chicken salad. Option: A slice of baked potato, which you should always have in the refrigerator, adds a delicious complement to this sandwich.

Dinner

Minestrone Soup

1 c. dried beans (navy, kidney,
    red, garbanzo, or a mixture)
¾ c. whole wheat macaroni
4 c. water
4 c. water, 5 bouillon cubes
1 c. fresh green beans
1 T. garlic, minced
1 small zucchini squash, diced
⅛ c. basil

1 c. shredded spinach or cabbage
1 c. diced tomatoes
1 c. finely diced carrots
1 c. chopped onions
1 c. chopped celery
½ c. finely chopped parsley
¼ t. rosemary
½ t. pepper
12 oz. tomato juice

To prepare dried beans, first soak overnight in 2 quarts of water. After soaking, place beans in pot with 2 cups water, cover and boil for 1 hour. Save the cooking liquid. In another large pan, saute all of the vegetables in a few tablespoons of bouillon. Place half the beans in a blender and puree. Add all the ingredients, except macaroni, to a large pot. Add the 2 cups of bean liquid and bring to a boil. Simmer for 45 minutes to an hour. Then add the macaroni and simmer 15 minutes or until the macaroni is tender. Serves 10 (1-cup servings). Add water to thin if necessary.

Italian Stuffed Green Peppers

4 large green peppers, cleaned

Sauce:
1 15-oz. can of tomatoes
4 T. fresh orange juice
¼ c. finely chopped celery
¼ clove garlic, crushed
¼ c. finely chopped onions

Stuffing:
2 c. cooked garbanzo beans with
  cooking liquid
2 c. cooked brown rice
¼ lb. ground beef
½ medium onion, chopped
2 egg whites
¼ c. finely chopped parsley
pepper, to taste
½ t. ground oregano
¼ t. anise
⅛ t. cumin

Sauce: Blend tomatoes in blender. Add remaining ingredients and simmer over low flame 5-10 minutes.

Stuffing: In a frying pan, cook ground beef, onion, parsley, pepper, oregano, anise and cumin, mixing thoroughly until cooked. Add brown rice to hamburger mixture and mix. Puree garbanzo beans in blender. Mix bean paste and egg whites with rice mixture, stir in half the sauce, and divide into 4 equal parts. Blanch each green pepper in boiling water for 15 seconds. Fill each pepper with stuffing, cover with remaining sauce and bake in baking dish in 350° oven for 45 minutes. Serves 4.

Blueberry Melba

4 T. low-fat yogurt
½ t. vanilla
4 peaches, cooked or
    water packed

1½ c. fresh or frozen blueberries
¼ c. apple juice

Mix vanilla and yogurt. In a glass cup place 1 tablespoon of vanilla yogurt. Top with one peach. Puree blueberries in a blender. If necessary add the apple juice to sweeten. Refrigerate both until fully chilled. Divide the blueberry sauce evenly on top of each fruit cup and serve. Serves 4.

Lunch

Cold Lentil Salad

¾ lb. dried red lentils
beef broth
1 c. chopped parsley
1 c. chopped onion

1 c. finely chopped red or
    green pepper
vinegar to taste

Wash lentils and place them in saucepan with enough water to cover. Cook the lentils for fifteen minutes, then drain. Refill saucepan with enough water or beef broth to cover lentils. Add pepper to taste. Slowly simmer the lentils until tender, about 40 minutes. Drain and chill the lentils. Before serving, mix in the parsley, onions, peppers, and season with vinegar. Serves 6.

Dinner

Sweet & Sour Bean Salad

2 c. dried garbanzo beans
2 c. dried kidney beans
1 10-oz. package frozen cut
    green beans
1 10-oz. package frozen cut
    wax beans

1 stalk celery, finely chopped
1 small onion, finely chopped
1 T. cider vinegar
2 T. apple juice
¼ t. ground oregano
1 t. lemon juice
1 garlic clove, crushed

Soak the dry beans overnight. Drain and cook beans separately in plenty of water, until tender (about 1-1½ hours). Drain. Cook the frozen beans until they are tender and drain. Combine everything in a deep bowl and toss thoroughly. Chill a few hours. Toss well just before serving. Serves 6.

Ratatouille Crepes

1 c. whole wheat pastry flour
1¼ c. skim milk

4 egg whites, stiffly beaten

Blend milk and flour until smooth, then carefully fold in the stiffly beaten egg whites. Heat a medium size non-stick pan until very hot. Pour in approximately ¼ cup of the batter so that it covers the bottom of the pan evenly. Cook the crepe on both sides until golden brown. Place 2-3 tablespoons ratatouille on each crepe and fold. Serve by topping each crepe with another tablespoon of ratatouille.

Dinner

Mexican Beef Stew

1 lb. top sirloin beef, cut
    into 1" cubes
3 c. water
1 c. tomato juice
4 medium tomatoes, chopped
4-6 T. finely chopped green
    chile, or to taste

1 t. chili powder
½ clove garlic, crushed
½ t. cumin
1 c. celery, cut into 1" pieces
1 large potato, peeled and cubed
½ c. chopped onions

Broil meat cubes on rack 3-4 inches from flame, turning until lightly browned. Place meat in skillet with the remaining ingredients and water. Cover and cook over low heat 1½ hours or until meat and vegetables are tender. Serves 4.

Pinto Beans

1 c. pinto beans   1 garlic clove

Fill pot with enough water so that water level is 2-3 inches above the beans. Bring water and beans to a boil and add whole peeled garlic clove. Add more water as needed. For best results cook for 4-5 hours until beans are almost mashed. Prepare ahead of time and refrigerate. Serves 4.

Banana Flambe

1 banana, cut in half lengthwise
¼ c. unsweetened apple juice
¼ t. vanilla
½ t. grated lemon rind

⅛ t. ground ginger
1 T. brandy
pinch of cinnamon

Place the banana slices in a large frying pan. Add the lemon rind, vanilla, apple juice and ginger. Cook over low heat for 3-5 minutes, continually basting it in its juices. Heat the brandy and pour it over the bananas. Ignite the brandy and shake the pan until the flames die out. Serve immediately. Serves 1.

Lunch

Potato Salad Sandwich

2 slices whole wheat bread,
 toasted
alfalfa sprouts
½ medium tomato, sliced thinly
2 slices green pepper
2 leaves romaine lettuce

1 thin slice purple onion
 (optional)
½ baked potato, thinly sliced
few pinches curry powder
2 T. yogurt
½ clove garlic, crushed
fresh ground pepper, to taste

Heap the vegetables onto one slice of the toasted bread. Top the pile with the baked potato slices. Mix the yogurt, garlic and curry powder and spread on the remaining toast. Assemble and eat. Serves 1.

Dinner

Broiled Fish with Lime Sauce

1 lb. boneless fish filets
3 T. low-fat yogurt
juice of ½ lime
6 t. finely chopped dill

½ clove garlic, crushed
fresh ground pepper, to taste
lime wedges

Place the fish in a non-stick baking dish. Mix the yogurt, garlic, lime juice and half the dill. Brush the sauce over the fish. Place fish under the broiler at 400°. Broil 10 minutes. Brush fish again with the remaining lime sauce and broil 5 minutes more. Sprinkle with remaining dill, garnish with lime wedges and serve. Serves 3.

Empress Vegetables

½ c. finely chopped
  green pepper
1 c. diced onion
1 c. fresh pineapple chunks
4 large carrots, thinly sliced
¼ t. ground ginger
½ t. vanilla

⅛ t. curry powder
¼ t. cinnamon
1 c. water chestnuts, sliced
½ c. cooked sweet potato,
  thinly sliced
½ banana, thinly sliced

Saute the green pepper in a few tablespoons of beef bouillon for 3 minutes in non-stick frying pan. Remove the green pepper and set aside. In the same pan, add ½ of the pineapple, the onions, vanilla, cinnamon, carrots, ginger and curry powder. Simmer until carrots are tender. Add the cooked green pepper, water chestnuts, banana, sweet potato and remaining pineapple. Cook 3-5 minutes and serve. Serves 4.

Brown Rice Parmigiana

2 shallots, chopped
1 small garlic clove, minced
½ c. chopped onions
1 c. brown rice

½ c. zucchini, diced
2 c. chicken bouillon
2 T. Parmesan cheese, grated

Add a few tablespoons of chicken bouillon to a non-stick frying pan and lightly saute garlic, zucchini, onions and shallots. Add rice to frying pan and saute while mixing it with the vegetables. Saute the rice until it begins to crackle. Bring the 2 cups of chicken broth to a rolling boil in a pot and add the rice mixture. Reduce rice to a simmer, cover, and cook for 45 minutes. Let cool 15 minutes. Toss lightly with Parmesan cheese and serve. Serves 4.

Lunch

Health Sandwich

2 slices whole wheat bread,
   toasted
¼ c. finely sliced mushrooms
¼ c. alfalfa sprouts
½ tomato, thinly sliced
1 thin slice Jack cheese

fresh ground pepper, to taste
oregano
1 t. low-fat yogurt
1 T. finely chopped green onion

Place the above ingredients on toast open-face in order given. Place in a microwave or under broiler 3-5 inches from flame until cheese melts. Top with second slice whole wheat toast. Optional: Top off with yogurt and green onions. Serves 1.

Dinner

Shish Kebob

1 lb. veal, lamb or beef
2 T. lemon juice
1 T. red wine vinegar
1 t. low salt soy sauce
1 clove garlic, minced
½ t. cumin

1 T. grated onion
1 t. crushed oregano leaves
20 mushroom caps
20 1-inch cubes of green pepper
20 1-inch cubes of onion
20 cherry tomatoes

Cube meat into 20 1-inch pieces. In a bowl, mix the vinegar, soy sauce, lemon juice, cumin and onion. Add the meat and let marinate overnight (at least 4 hours). Reserve the marinade. Skewer the mushrooms, meat, onion, tomatoes and green pepper in that order. Each skewer should hold 5 pieces of vegetables, 5 pieces of meat and 5 mushrooms each. Grill kebobs under broiler 4 inches from heat source or over a charcoal grill for 10-15 minutes or to desired doneness. Baste with marinade. Sprinkle with a pinch or two of crushed oregano and serve. Serves 4.

Curry Rice

1 c. brown rice	1-2 T. curry
1 apple, diced	2 c. water

Bring water to a boil. Add brown rice and return to boil. Now add apple and 1-2 tablespoons curry. Stir well. Add more curry is desired. Simmer covered for 45 minutes. Serves 4.

Lunch

Tuna Salad Sandwich

2 slices whole wheat bread,
   toasted
2 oz. tuna salad
   (see Plunge)
lettuce
tomato

1 thin slice onion
½ c. alfalfa sprouts
1 thin slice green pepper
2 T. salad dressing of choice
   (see Sauces, Marinades, etc.
   sections)

Set the vegetables on one slice of toast and top with tuna salad. Spread salad dressing over the other slice and assemble. Option: Use garlic toast.

Onion Soup

4 onions, thinly sliced
4 c. beef bouillon

2 T. sherry

Place onions and ½ cup of bouillon in a saucepan, cover and simmer 10 minutes. Stir occasionally until liquid evaporates. Add the remaining bouillon and simmer for 25 minutes. Add the sherry and simmer 5 minutes more. Serves 4.

Dinner

Zucchini and Pasta

4 oz. whole wheat pasta
1½ c. thinly sliced zucchini
1 c. whole canned tomatoes,
   diced
1 T. tomato paste
¼ c. chopped onion

½ c. thinly sliced
   fresh mushrooms
½ garlic clove, minced
2 t. red wine
2 T. Parmesan cheese, grated
pepper to taste

Combine all the ingredients except the pasta in a non-stick frying pan. Simmer over medium heat for 30 minutes or until zucchini is tender and juicy. Add 1 or 2 tablespoons of water to retain moisture, if necessary. Cook pasta and drain. Serve zucchini sauce over pasta. Top each serving with 1 tablespoon of Parmesan. Serves 2.

Herbed Carrots

8 oz. carrots
1 T. beef bouillon

⅛ t. thyme
pepper to taste

Cut carrots into 1" pieces. Set pieces on a 8" square piece of aluminum foil. Mix bouillon, thyme and pepper and spoon over carrots. Wrap foil completely around carrots and bake in 350° oven for 1 hour. Serves 2.

Lunch

Pocket Pizza

¼ c. diced zucchini
2 oz. ground beef
2-⅛″ horizontal slices of
    eggplant
3 T. chopped onion
½ clove garlic, minced
¼ t. anise (option, for Italian
    sausage flavor)

¼ t. oregano, ground
1 whole wheat pita bread
1 T. Parmesan cheese, grated
2 oz. tomato sauce
1 t. red wine
1 oz. tomato paste

Place the ground beef in a non-stick pan with onions, anise and garlic. Bring to a simmer. At the same time place the eggplant slices on a non-stick cookie sheet and bake in a 350° oven until dry (10-15 minutes); remove from oven. Add the zucchini to the hamburger and continue frying until the zucchini is tender. Stir in the tomato sauce and paste; continue stirring for 1-2 minutes over low heat. When completely mixed, add the oregano and red wine and continue stirring. If necessary, add a couple of tablespoons of water to keep moist. Cut off the very top of the pita bread and stuff with the oven cooked eggplant. Add the meat mixture, sprinkle with Parmesan and eat. Note: May be re-heated in the oven or eaten for lunch at room temperature. Serves 1.

Dinner

Garlic Soup

2 leeks, white and light green
only, trimmed, cleaned
and sliced
15-20 cloves garlic, peeled
and stem removed
6 c. chicken bouillon

6 medium potatoes, peeled
and cubed
1 c. skim milk
1½ c. small whole wheat bread
croutons

Add ½ cup bouillon, leeks and garlic to pot. Cook on medium heat for 2-3 minutes, stirring constantly. Add remaining bouillon and potatoes and bring to a boil. Cover and simmer for 45 minutes. Strain out garlic cloves and potatoes. Reserve soup broth. Gradually strain and press all juices from garlic into soup broth. Puree potatoes with 1 cup soup broth in blender. Return potato puree to broth and simmer 5-10 minutes. Add skim milk and heat to boil. Serve with croutons.

Serves 6.

Sweet Cabbage Rolls

1 large cabbage
Filling:
4 oz. ground beef
½ c. brown rice
½ c. diced onions

4 T. finely diced green pepper
½ c. finely diced celery
2 canned tomatoes, diced
2 T. raisins
3 T. apple juice

Cook the rice in 2 cups of water until done (45 minutes). Place the ground beef into a non-stick skillet and brown. Add diced tomatoes, onions, green pepper and garlic. Simmer for 10 minutes, adding a tablespoon of water to retain moisture if necessary. Add the raisins and rice and mix thoroughly. Set aside. Prepare the sauce (see chili relleno sauce, p. 150). Place the whole cabbage in a large pot of boiling water and cover. The leaves should separate in 15-20 minutes. Separate cabbage leaves. Divide the filling into 6 equal parts and fill six medium sized leaves. Place the filling in the center of each leaf and fold up securely. Hold with a toothpick if necessary. Set rolls seam-side down in a non-stick baking pan and bake at 350° for 45 minutes. Pour sauce over rolls and serve. Serves 2.

Camden Drive Quiche

Hannah's Cheese
  (Use the amount yielded
  in recipe in Chapter 17)
4 T. undiluted frozen apple
  juice concentrate

Whole wheat pie crust
  (Available at
  health food stores)
4 egg whites

Prepare Hannah's cheese. Place it in a bowl and break into small pieces. Beat egg whites until soft peaks form. Add the egg whites and apple juice. Mix well. Turn mixture into a whole wheat pie crust shell and bake at 350 degrees for 35 minutes. Cool ten minutes and cut into six portion sizes or 12 snack size wedges.

CHAPTER SEVENTEEN:

EXTRA SAUCES, DIPS, DRESSINGS, AND MARINADES

SAUCES

A tablespoon of these low-cal, low-salt, low-fat specialties will give wonderful zest to fish, chicken, vegetables, etc. They provide a wider choice of taste-enhancers for either the Plunge or Everyday recipes.

Catsup

1 c. whole canned tomatoes	pinch dry mustard
3 T. tomato paste, unsalted	¼ t. finely minced garlic clove
1 T. vinegar	pinch black pepper
1 T. orange juice	cloves
¼ c. finely chopped onion	

Combine tomatoes, tomato paste and onion in a saucepan and simmer for 30 minutes. Pour this mixture into blender and puree. Return puree to saucepan and add remaining ingredients. Simmer and stir until flavors marry (10-15 minutes).

Yield: 1 cup.

Note: For barbeque sauce, increase mustard to ¼ t., add 1 t. chili powder, 1 T. orange juice and 4 T. Worcestershire sauce.

Red Chile Sauce

2 c. whole canned tomatoes
3 T. tomato paste
3 oz. canned green chiles,
    finely diced
½ c. finely diced fresh tomato

⅛ t. ground oregano
½ t. garlic, crushed
1 T. cilantro (optional, see Hints)
¼ c. finely diced onions

Combine canned tomatoes, tomato paste and onions in a saucepan and simmer for 30 minutes. Pour this mixture into blender and puree. Add the remaining ingredients and chill before serving.
Yield: 2 cups.

Curry Sauce

2 c. chicken or beef bouillon
2 t. curry powder
⅛ t. dry mustard

1 T. undiluted frozen apple juice
1 T. cornstarch
¼ small garlic clove, crushed

Combine curry powder, mustard, apple juice and garlic clove in a saucepan. Simmer briefly, mix and set aside. Bring the bouillon to a boil in a non-stick pan. Dissolve the cornstarch in 1 T. of water. Add this slowly to bouillon, stirring until it thickens. Stir in remaining curry mixture and serve.
Yield: 2 cups.

Spaghetti Sauce (All-purpose Italian sauce)

4 c. whole canned tomatoes,
    finely chopped (Italian
    plum are the best)
½ c. tomato paste
1 garlic clove, finely minced
1 t. oregano

1 c. fresh mushrooms,
    finely chopped
½ c. diced celery
¼ c. diced onions
1 T. red wine (optional)
3 T. shredded carrot

Combine all ingredients in a non-stick frying pan. Bring to a boil. Reduce to a simmer and cook for 30-60 minutes, stirring regularly. Add water to thin, if needed.
Yield: 5 cups.

Sweet and Sour Sauce

¼ medium green pepper, diced
2 oz. green onions
1½ c. canned tomatoes
1 t. fresh ginger, grated
1 garlic clove, finely minced
¼ t. mustard
2 T. vinegar

4 t. Worcestershire
½ c. crushed pineapple, packed
   in water or no sugar added
2 T. orange juice, undiluted
2 t. cornstarch or arrowroot
pepper to taste (freshly ground
   is better)

Puree tomatoes in blender. Place all ingredients except cornstarch or arrowroot in a non-stick saucepan. Cook uncovered over medium heat for 10 minutes, stirring constantly. Mix cornstarch in cold water and stir into mixture until it thickens. Remove from heat. Use on broiled chicken, fish and Chinese vegetable dishes.

Yield: 2½-3 cups

White Wine Sauce

1 c. skim milk
1 T. dry white wine

1 T. arrowroot
1 shallot, minced

Mix 2 T. milk with arrowroot and set aside. Bring the remaining milk to a boil. When it starts to foam reduce heat to a simmer. Add the arrowroot paste, shallots and white wine, stirring until thickened. Simmer for 2-3 minutes. Serve. Use over chicken, fish and steamed vegetables.

Yield: 1 cup.

Mustard Cream Sauce

½ c. low-fat yogurt
2 T. fresh orange juice
2 T. white wine vinegar
1 t. white wine

1 t. chopped dill
½ t. curry powder
¼ t. tarragon

Mix all ingredients. Chill. Use on broiled fish, chicken and as a cold vegetable dip.

Yield: ½ cup.

Teriyaki Sauce/Marinade

½ c. soy sauce
(salt reduced type)
1 small clove garlic, minced
1 t. ground ginger
1 T. unsweetened orange juice,
undiluted

½ c. water
½ c. lemon juice in ½ c. club soda
1 bay leaf

Combine all ingredients. Sauce: use immediately. Marinade: several hours or overnight.

1 T. = 4 calories.

DIPS

Curry Dip

1 c. mock sour cream
½ clove garlic, minced
1 T. fresh parsley,
finely chopped
1 T. lemon juice

¼ t. paprika
½ t. curry powder, or to taste
¼ t. horseradish, or to taste

Mix together all ingredients. Chill. Excellent for party dip with crudites.
1 T. = 7.5 calories.

185

Eggplant Dip

1 medium eggplant	1 small onion, finely diced
3 T. fresh parsley,	2 medium tomatoes, finely diced
finely chopped	1 t. cumin
1 small clove garlic, crushed	½ t. fresh ground pepper
¼ c. lemon juice	

Bake whole eggplant in a 350° oven 45-60 minutes, or until it is soft. Peel eggplant and cut into sections. Add eggplant and half of the tomatoes to blender. Blend until smooth. Pour into serving bowl. Mix together the remaining ingredients and add them to eggplant puree. Toss. Chill.

Note: Add more spices and/or lemon juice to taste. Excellent party dip, expecially with whole wheat pita bread for dipping.

Total calories: 215.

Mexican Bean Dip

2 c. cooked pinto beans	1 onion, finely diced
2-3 oz. canned green chile,	1 t. chili powder
chopped	pinch of cumin, to taste

Mash the beans in a saucepan and thin over a low flame with a tablespoon or two of water to desired dip consistency. Mix in remaining ingredients and serve.

1 T. = 17 calories: ¼ cup = 68 calories.

Hannah's Cheese

6 c. milk   **1⅓ c. lowfat yogurt**

Heat six cups skim milk to boiling. Drop in the yogurt. When in 2-3 minutes there is a separation (white curds on top and yellow whey below) turn all into a colander and let drain. Press out most of the liquid with a wooden spoon or your hands. Voila! You now have cheese. For dips and stuffings take the cheese and blend with any of the following or combination thereof: parsley, fresh garlic, celery seeds, chopped chives, horseradish. For dips add skim milk and blend until smooth.

DRESSINGS

Thousand Island Dressing

1 c. mock sour cream   **1 T. onion, grated**
4 T. catsup   **½ t. paprika**
1 T. green pepper,   **⅛ t. chili powder**
finely chopped

Blend all ingredients. Use skim milk to thin. Chill. Makes 1¼ cups.
1 T. = 6 calories.

French Dressing

1 small cucumber, chopped   **1 c. tarragon vinegar**
1 small onion, chopped   **1 small garlic clove, crushed**
½ tomato, finely diced   **¼ t. Dijon mustard**
1 c. water   **¼ t. horseradish**
                                ½ t. fresh ground pepper

Combine cucumber, onion, tomato, and water in blender and puree. Add remaining ingredients and blend until smooth. Chill. Yields: 2⅓-3 cups.
1 T. = 5 calories.

Spicy Lemon Dressing

2 T. grated lemon peel
½ c. lemon juice (fresh)
2 cloves garlic, minced
   or crushed
½ t. ground coriander

½ t. ground cumin
½ t. dry mustard
½ t. paprika
1 T. apple juice unsweetened
   and undiluted
freshly ground pepper to taste

In a covered jar combine all ingredients. Shake well. Let stand at room temperature for at least an hour until the flavors marry. Shake well before using.

1 T. = 7 calories.

MARINADES

All Purpose Beef Marinade

½ c. tarragon red wine vinegar
1 small clove garlic, crushed
¼ c. chives, finely chopped

½ t. thyme
¼ t. oregano leaves

Mix together all ingredients. To marinate several pieces, place this marinade and meat in a plastic bag and seal. Turn the bag occasionally, coating all pieces at the same time.

All Purpose Chicken Marinade

½ c. chicken bouillon
2 T. dry white wine
¼ t. oregano leaves

¼ clove garlic, crushed
1 T. fresh parsley

Mix together all ingredients. Follow the same procedure as with the beef marinade with plastic bag. For variations add 1 teaspoon of grated lemon rind. Also try marinating chicken in teriyaki sauce.

CHAPTER EIGHTEEN:

MAINTENANCE: PERMANENT WEIGHT LOSS, THE LONG-LIFE ANTI-STRESS PROGRAM

CONGRATULATIONS!

You've won!

You've finally achieved your goal. For years perhaps you've been wanting to look the way you do now. Forgotten are the torments your unwanted fat used to cause you. You have lost five, ten, twenty, thirty, or more pounds. You are excused if you like to linger in front of the mirror and admire the new figure you see there. You have reason to be proud of yourself.

Yet, as pleased as you are, this is not yet the time to rest on your laurels. In fact, the real battle is just beginning. You are now entering upon the actual Long-Life and Anti-Stress part of the BHMD. Your weight loss and the nutritional practices you have developed in the process are now to be carried forward into the routine of your daily life. You have learned that sound nutrition is the key to stress and proper weight maintenance. This chapter tells you how to implement your knowledge on a permanent basis.

Though the Maintenance allows you greater latitude in eating, the BHMD principles hold true for this program as much as they did for the Plunge and the Everyday plans. Your diet will still emphasize the Complex Carbohydrates and minimize the protein and fats. But because rapid

189

weight loss is no longer in order, a few and occasional digressions are permitted. These pertain chiefly to the use of fats, oils, cheeses and egg yolks.

STRICT MODERATION

The policy on fats, oils and cheeses is simple. Don't gobble them wholesale. Don't pour them into your sauces and gravies as you were wont to do in the fattening days of yore. Use them as flavoring agents. And then only in *strict moderation*.

Many recipes from the BHMD lend themselves excellently to this approach. When preparing your meals you may want to integrate a teaspoon or two of oils for flavor. Always get the best available: oilve oil, sweet unsalted butter, tahini, or sesame oil.

A teaspoon of sesame oil, for instance, will certainly enrich almost any Chinese dish, such as Szechuan Beef Salad or Sweet Sour Chicken. Similarly, just a teaspoon of butter or olive oil may enhance a fish dish or an Italian recipe. The key as always is *strict moderation*. Let the teaspoon rather than the cup or ladle be your measure.

On the Maintenance program the slight use of fats and oils to flavor your dishes will not contravene the principles of healthful eating that are the basis of the BHMD. With its general high-Complex Carbohydrate approach, the BHMD restores the nutritional balance to a diet sprinkled with very moderate amounts of oils and fats. But anything more than a teaspoon of oil and fat daily will undo much of the sound nutrition to which the BHMD is dedicated. All the serious possibilities related to poor nutrition, such as heart disease and cancer, will again crop up if the strict guidelines on fats and oils are consistently violated.

For cheese the same rules apply. Though one of man's finest palate pleasers, most of the delicious cheeses are high in calories and fat. Therefore, use cheese sparingly, preferably as a flavoring agent. A tablespoon of Fontina melted over Veal Marsala, or an extra tablespoon of Parmesan over pasta and vegetables won't destroy your new dieting habits. The danger comes only with excess.

190

The Long-Life Anti-Stress Program:
WHAT YOU SHOULD EAT

The remainder of this chapter is a capsule directory that will keep you on my Long-Life Anti-Stress Program. From my experience in counseling patients I have assembled the basic nutritional guidelines for eliminating the chief *stressors* from the average American diet. By adhering closely to the following guidelines you will keep at bay such stressors on your health as fats, processed foods, sugars and salt.

This information is also a guide to the most wholesome ingredients you can eat to maintain health and wellbeing. And remember: you're always shooting for no more than 1,500-2,000 calories a day!

- Eat less red meat (beef, veal, lamb, pork).
- Eat fish more often for animal protein (see Fish Hints).
- Eat more turkey and chicken.
- Remove poultry skin before cooking.
- Eliminate fried foods at home and when eating out.
- Learn to cook without fats or oils - bake, broil, steam, poach.
- Eliminate restaurant hamburgers, hot dogs, breaded fresh fish, and delicatessen meats (cold cuts, pastrami, corned beef, etc.).
- Use little or no butter, and *certainly* no margarine.
- Use non-fat milk and buttermilk–no whole milk, no low-fat milk, no cream, no whipped cream, no sour cream.
- Use hoop cheese (skim milk cheese with no added salt).
- For slicing and melting cheese, use part skim milk cheese (string, mozzarella, etc.) One ounce a day only.
- Use plain low fat yogurt in place of sour cream (on a baked potato for example), or one of the BHMD-type salad dressings.
- Nuts and seeds contain a large percentage of fats. They should be eaten fresh and raw only. One ounce a day only.
- For salad dressings, learn to use lemon juice or vinegar.

LOW FAT EATING

The following foods are low in fat:

Apples
Apricots
Artichokes
Asparagus
Bananas
Barley
Beets
Berries
Black beans
Broccoli
Brown rice
Buckwheat
Buttermilk
Cabbage
Carrots
Cauliflower
Celery
Cherries
Chestnuts
Chicken, white, no skin
Cilantro
Cod
Corn
Cranberries
Cress, water and garden
Cucumbers
Dandelion greens
Eggplant
Endive
Flounder
Garbanzos
Garlic
Grapefruit
Haddock
Halibut
Hoop cheese
Jerusalem artichokes
Jicama
Kale
Kidney beans
Kohlrabi
Lentils
Lettuce, dark green
Lobster
Lychee nuts
Mangos
Melons
Milk, skim or 1% fat

Millet
Mushrooms
Mustard greens
Nectarines
Oats
Okra
Onions, all kinds
Oranges
Papayas
Parsley
Parsnips
Peaches
Pears
Peas
Peppers, all kinds
Perch
Pike
Pineapple
Pink Beans
Plantains
Plums
Popcorn
Potatoes
Pumpkin
Radish
Red beans
Red snapper
Rutabagas
Whole grain rye
Sand dabs
Scallops, steamed
Sea bass
Shrimp
Sole
Spinach
Split peas
Sprouts, all kinds
Sweet potatoes
Tangerines
Tomatoes
Tuna, in water
Turkey, white, no skin
Turnips
Whole grain wheat
White beans
Wild rice

DON'T EAT PROCESSED FOODS, SUCH AS
WHITE FLOUR

Just look at what is removed from the whole wheat kernel to make white flour:

94% of the pyridoxine (B6)	57% of the pantothenic acid
66% of the riboflavin (B2)	60% of the calcium
74% of the potassium	78% of the magnesium
50% of the linoleic acid	97% of the thiamine (B1)
27% of the protein	76% of the iron

DO EAT

UNPROCESSED WHOLE GRAINS

Barley	Whole grain oats
Brown rice	Whole grain rye
Buckwheat	Whole grain wheat
Corn	Wild rice
Millet	

- Whole grains are rich sources of B vitamins, minerals, fibers, and good low fat protein, as well as Complex Carbohydrates.
- Use whole grains as cereal and casseroles. Use breads made of *all* whole grain.
- Four servings every day (or according to your weight).
  One serving = one slice bread.
  One serving = ½ cup cooked serving grain.
- See the recipes.

LEGUMES

- Legumes are dried beans and peas.

Black beans	Lima beans
Garbanzos	Pinto beans
Great Northern beans	Red beans
Kidney beans	Small white beans
Lentils	Split peas

- Legumes are high in vitamin B1, B6, and other vitamins; high in minerals such as calcium and iron; high in fiber, and contain up to 20% protein, and are also low in fat.
- Make chili beans, lentil stew, split pea soup.
- Eat up to ½ cup cooked beans or peas for lunch or dinner — eat even more if you are growing or are skinny.

FRUITS

Apples
Apricots
Bananas
Berries (all kinds)
Cherries
Citrus fruits
Figs
Grapes
Guavas

Mangos
Melons (all kinds)
Peaches
Pears
Persimmons
Pineapple
Plums
Pomegranates
Tomatoes

- Fruits are packed with vitamins, minerals, and sweetness!
- Eat whole fruit, not fruit juices.
- Eat raw fruit, not cooked, canned or frozen.
- Eat fresh fruit, not dried. (Occasionally allowable as a confection.)
- Eat two to four fruits a day, according to your weight and sugar sensitivity.

VEGETABLES

Artichokes
Asparagus
Beets
Broccoli
Brussels sprouts
Cabbage, red & green
Carrots
Cauliflower
Celery
Chard
Cilantro
Cucumbers
Eggplant
Garlic
Jicama
Kohlrabi
Leeks

Lettuce (especially dark green)
Mushrooms
Okra
Onions (Bermuda, white, green, shallots and chives.)
Parsley
Parsnips
Peas
Peppers, green, red and yellow
Potatoes, red and white
Radishes
Rutabagas
Spinach
Sprouts, alfalfa, bean & others
Squash, all kinds
Turnips
Watercress

- Vegetables are sources for many vitamins, minerals and enzymes, as well as a good source of dietary fiber.
- A diet including many vegetables lowers blood fats.
- When you cook vegetables, cook for as short a time as possible — just until they are tender and crisp.
- Use more raw than cooked vegetables. Cooking destroys many vitamins and minerals.
- Eat at least four large servings a day.
- The huge selection of vegetables adds variety and appeal to every meal.

NUTS

Almonds	Hazelnuts
Cashews	Lychee (low in fat)
Chestnuts (low in fat)	Pecans
Filberts	Walnuts

- Nuts are high in fats so you cannot eat many — six to eight a day at the most.
- To protect the delicate poly-unsaturated fatty acids in nuts, use the nuts raw (not roasted, dry roasted or salted).

SEEDS

Anise	Poppy
Caraway	Psyllium
Chia	Sesame
Celery	Sunflower
Dill	Pumpkin
Flax	

- Seeds are high in poly-unsaturated fats.
- Use seeds fresh and raw.
- Use small amounts of seeds for crunch and flavor· in cooked grains and cereals, casseroles, salads.
- One to two tablespoons a day.

DAIRY PRODUCTS

- Skim or buttermilk, if desired. Eight ounces a day, minumum.
- If you like yogurt, eat plain, low fat yogurt. Better yet, make your own non-fat yogurt at home. Two to four ounces a day.
- Use yogurt instead of sour cream and mayonnaise. See our recipes.
- Cheese is high in fat and salt. Use hoop cheese, up to 4 ounces a day.

FISH

- *FIN FISH*

Brook Trout	Pike
Cod	Red Snapper
Flounder	Sand Dabs
Haddock	Seabass
Halibut	Sole
Perch	Tuna (if canned, use water packed without salt)

- *SHELL FISH*

Abalone	Mussels
Clams	Oysters
Crab	Scallop
Lobster	Shrimp

(Low in total fat, but higher in cholesterol than fin fish).

- The lowest fat source of animal protein as well as an important vitamin & mineral source.

FOWL

White meat without skin:

Chicken   Turkey

- The second lowest fat source of animal protein; also supplies vitamins and minerals (but usually in lower quantities than seafood).
- 5 to 6 ounces a day will supply sufficient protein.

WATER

- You Need Water! Drink plenty of water; your body will not operate efficiently without it. At least five eight-ounce glasses a day.

FRESH FOODS

- In all of the food groups, make fresh foods your first choice. They look better, taste better, and are more nutritious.

FIBER

All natural, unprocessed whole grains, dry beans, and peas contain fiber in good amounts.

For comparison:

To get 2 gms. of crude fiber, you would have to eat:
  2 tablespoons of bran, or *1 cup* of All Bran Packaged Cereal
  3 oz. whole wheat bread, or *2 pounds* of white bread
Meat contains 0% fiber.
Milk contains 0% fiber.
Cheese contains 0% fiber.

For natural, whole food, high-fiber eating, look to:

Buckwheat	9.9% fiber
Garbanzo beans	5.0% fiber
Dry peas	4.9% fiber
Lentils	3.9% fiber
Popcorn	2.2% fiber
Whole wheat bread	1.9% fiber
White beans	1.6% fiber
Red beans	1.5% fiber
Oatmeal	1.2% fiber

196

GUIDE TO LOW SUGAR EATING

- Honey, maple syrup, molasses are simple carbohydrates without fiber. Avoid them all.
- Fructose, brown, raw and turbinado sugars are like white sugar - without fiber. Avoid them all.
- Avoid processed, canned, frozen, prepared, packaged foods. Many contain sugars under other names such as:

sucrose	maltose
fructose	dextrose
glucose	corn syrup
lactose	invert sugar
honey	maple syrup
molasses	brown, raw, turbinado sugar

- Not only dessert foods, but canned soups, vegetables and fruits, bouillon cubes, catsup, cereals, non-dairy creamers, etc., etc., may contain the above sugars.
- Avoid obviously sweetened foods - bakery goods, frozen yogurt, yogurt with fruit and honey or sugar, ice cream, soft drinks, candy, etc., etc.
- Do not drink fruit juice - juice is the high sugar (fructose) content of the fruit without the naturally occurring fiber. Also, the juice that most people drink is canned, bottled, or frozen which means it was cooked at one time.
- Do not use cooked fruit — too many vitamins and minerals are destroyed in the cooking process.
- Use dried fruit as a confection - no more than one ounce daily.
- Do not have sweets in your house - avoid temptation. Don't forget - sweets can be addictive: The less you eat, the less you crave!
- Do not use artificial sweeteners - why add a possibly dangerous chemical to your diet? Learn to enjoy the natural goodness of grains, fruits and vegetables. Men who smoke greatly increase their chance of bladder cancer if they use artificial sweeteners.

GUIDE TO LOW SALT EATING

Interesting notes:

Fresh tuna - 100 gm.	1.3 mg. sodium
Canned tuna in water - 100 gm. (salt added)	875.0 mg. sodium
Fresh asparagus - 8 oz.	39.5 mg. sodium
Canned asparagus - 8 oz. (salt added)	865.0 mg. sodium
Fresh peas - 8 oz.	1.0 mg. sodium
Frozen peas - 8 oz.	121.0 mg. sodium
Canned peas - 8 oz.	204.0 mg. sodium

The sodium in fresh foods is good for you. The salt in processed, canned, frozen, pre-cooked, etc., foods is not!

- Cottage cheese has salt added; there is no salt added to hoop cheese. The sodium in hoop cheese is naturally in the milk.

  ½ cup cottage cheese contains .... 453 mg. sodium
  ½ cup hoop cheese contains .... 262 mg. sodium
- One teaspoon salt contains .... 2,132 mg. sodium
  One tablespoon soy sauce contains .... 1,319 mg. sodium
- The human body was not designed to ingest this much sodium. Eat the sodium nature gives you - *and no more!*

CALORIE CHART

MILK, CHEESE, CREAM, IMITATION CREAM; RELATED PRODUCTS   Calories

Milk:
  Fluid:
    Nonfat (skim), 1 cup 90
  Dry, nonfat instant:
    Low-density, 1 cup 245
Buttermilk:
  Fluid, cultured, made
    from skim milk, 1 cup 90
Cheese, natural:
  Cheddar, 1 cup 115
  Cottage, large or small curd,
    uncreamed (curd pressed
    down), 1 cup 170
  Parmesan, grated:
    1 tablespoon 25
    1 ounce 130
  Swiss, 1 oz 105

Sour dressing (imitation sour
cream) made with nonfat
dry milk, 1 cup 440
           1 tablespoon 20
Yogurt:
  Made from partially
    skimmed milk, 1 cup 125
  Made from whole milk, 1 cup 150

EGGS

Eggs, large, 24 ounces per dozen:
  White of egg, 1 white 15

MEAT, POULTRY, FISH, SHELLFISH, RELATED PRODUCTS

Beef, cooked:
  Cuts braised, simmered,
  or pot-roasted:
    Lean and fat, 3 oz. 245
    Lean only, 2.5 oz 140
  Hamburger (ground beef), broiled:
    Lean, 3 oz. 185
    Regular, 3 oz 245

Roast, oven-cooked, no liquid
added:
  Relatively fat, such as rib:
    Lean and fat, 3 oz. 375
    Lean only, 1.8 oz 125
  Relatively lean, such as
  heel of round:
    Lean and fat, 3 oz. 165
    Lean only, 2.7 oz 125

Steak, broiled:
  Relatively fat, such as sirloin:
    Lean and fat, 3 oz. 330
    Lean only, 2.0 oz 115
  Relatively lean, such as round:
    Lean and fat, 3 oz. 220
    Lean only, 2.4 oz 130

Chicken, cooked:
  Flesh only, broiled, 3 oz 115
  Breast, fried, ½ breast:
    With bone, 3.3 oz. 155
    Flesh and skin only, 2.7 oz. 155
  Chicken, canned, boneless, 3 oz 170

Lamb, cooked:
  Chop, thick, with bone, 1 chop ... 400
    Lean only, 2.6 oz 140
  Leg, roasted:
    Lean only, 2.5 oz 130
  Shoulder, roasted:
    Lean only, 2.3 oz 130

Veal, medium fat, cooked,
bone removed:
  Cutlet, 3 oz. 185
  Roast, 3 oz. 230

Fish and shellfish:
  Bluefish, baked with
    table fat, 3 oz. 135
  Crabmeat, canned, 3 oz. 85
  Haddock, 4 oz 100
  Ocean perch, 4 oz. 155
  Salmon, pink, canned, 3 oz. 120
  Shrimp, canned, meat, 3 oz 100
  Tuna, canned in water, 6 oz 220

MATURE DRY BEANS AND PEAS, NUTS, PEANUTS; RELATED PRODUCTS

Almonds, shelled, whole
kernels, 1 cup 850
Beans, dry:
  Common varieties as Great
  Northern, navy, and others:
    Cooked, drained:
      Great Northern, 1 cup 210
      Navy (pea), 1 cup 225
    Canned, solids and liquid:
      Red kidney, 1 cup 230
    Lima, cooked, drained, 1 cup ... 260

Coconut, fresh, meat only:
  Pieces, approx. 2x2x½ inch,
    1 piece 155
  Shredded or grated, firmly,
    packed, 1 cup 450

Cowpeas or blackeye peas,
dry, cooked, 1 cup............... 190

Peanuts, roasted, salted,
halves, 1 cup.................... 840
Peanut butter, 1 tablespoon....... 95
Peas, split, dry, cooked, 1 cup 290
Pecans, halves, 1 cup 740
Walnuts, black or native,
chopped, 1 cup.................. 790

VEGETABLES AND VEGETABLE PRODUCTS

Asparagus, green:
  Cooked, drained:
    Spears, ½-inch diam.
    at base, 4 spears, ... 10
    Pieces, 1½-2-in. lengths, 1 cup ... 30
    Canned, solids and
    liquid, 1 cup 45
Beans:
  Lima, immature seeds,
  cooked and drained, 1 cup....... 190
  Snap:
    Green:
      Cooked, drained, 1 cup 30
      Canned, solids, and
      liquid, 1 cup 45
    Yellow or wax:
      Cooked, drained, 1 cup 30
      Canned, solids and
      liquid, 1 cup 45
Sprouted mung beans, cooked
drained, 1 cup................... 35

Beets:
  Cooked, drained, peeled:
    Whole beets, 2-in. diam.
    2 beets...................... 30
    Diced or sliced, 1 cup........... 55
    Canned, solids and
    liquids, 1 cup 85
Beet greens, leaves and stems,
cooked, drained, 1 cup 25

Blackeye peas – see Cowpeas

Broccoli, cooked, drained:
  Whole stalks, medium size,
  1 stalk 45
  Stalks cut into ½-in. pieces,
  1 cup 40
  Chopped, yield from 10-oz. frozen
  pkg., 1⅜ cups 65

Brussels sprouts, 7-8 sprouts
(1¼-1½-in. diam.) per cup,
cooked, 1 cup................... 55
Cabbage:
  Common varieties:
    Raw:
      Coarsely shredded, 1 cup...... 15
      Finely shredded or
      chopped, 1 cup............... 20
      Cooked, 1 cup 30

Red, raw, coarsely shredded,
1 cup 20
Savoy, raw, coarsely shredded,
1 cup 15
Cabbage, celery or Chinese, raw,
cut in 1-in. pieces, 1 cup 10
Cabbage, spoon (or pakchoy),
cooked, 1 cup.................... 25
Carrots:
  Raw:
    Whole, 5½x1-in., 1 carrot
    (25 thin strips) 20
    Grated, 1 cup................. 45
  Cooked, diced, 1 cup 45
  Canned, strained or chopped,
  (baby food), 1 oz. 10
Cauliflower, cooked,
flowerbuds, 1 cup 25

Celery, raw:
  Stalk, large outer 8 by about 1½-in.
  at root end, 1 stalk 5
  Pieces, diced, 1 cup 15
Collards, cooked, 1 cup 55

Corn, sweet:
  Cooked, ear 5x1¾-in., 1 ear 70
  Canned, solids and liquid, 1 cup ... 170

Cowpeas, cooked, immature
seeds, 1 cup 175

Cucumbers, 10-oz., 7½x2-in.:
  Raw, pared, 1 cucumber 30
  Raw, pared, center slice
  ⅛-in. thick, 6 slices 5

Dandelion greens, cooked, 1 cup.... 60
Endive, curly (including
escarole), 2 oz................... 10
Kale, leaves including stems,
cooked, 1 cup................... 30
Lettuce, raw:
  Butterhead, as Boston types;
  head, 4-in. diam., 1 head........ 30
  Crisphead, as Iceberg;
  head, 4¾-in. diam., 1 head 60
  Looseleaf, or bunching varieties,
  leaves, 2 large 10

Mushrooms, canned, solids
and liquid, 1 cup 40
Mustard greens, cooked, 1 cup.... 35

Okra, cooked, pod 3x⅝-in.,
8 pods 25
Onions:
  Mature:
    Raw, onion 2½ diam., 1 onion ... 40
    Cooked, 1 cup 60
  Young, green, small, without
  tops, 6 onions.................. 20

Parsley, raw, chopped,
1 tablespoon ....Trace
Parsnips, cooked, 1 cup 100

Peas, green:
Cooked, 1 cup 115
Canned, solids and
liquid, 1 cup 165
Canned, strained,
(baby food), 1 oz. 15

Peppers, hot, red without
seeds, dried (ground chili powder,
added seasonings), 1 tablespoon... 50
Peppers, sweet:
Raw, about 5 per lb:
Green pod without stem and
seeds, 1 pod 15
Cooked, boiled, drained, 1 pod... 15

Potatoes, medium (about 3 per
pound raw):
Baked, peeled after baking,
1 potato .... 90 Boiled:
Peeled after boiling,
1 potato 105
Peeled before boiling, 1 potato ... 80
Potato chips, medium,
2-in. diam., 10 chips 115

Pumpkin, canned, 1 cup 75

Radishes, raw, small,
without tops, 4 radishes 5

Sauerkraut, canned, solids
and liquid, 1 cup 45

Spinach:
Cooked, 1 cup 40
Canned, drained solids, 1 cup.... 45

Squash:
Cooked:
Summer, diced, 1 cup 30
Winter, baked, mashed
1 cup 130

Sweet Potatoes:
Cooked, medium, 5x2-in., weight
raw about 6 oz.:
Baked, peeled after baking,
1 sweet potato 155
Boiled, peeled after boiling,
1 sweet potato 170
Candied, 3½x2¼-in.,
1 sweet potato 295
Canned, vacuum or solid pack,
1 cup 235

Tomatoes:
Raw, approx. 3-in. diam. 2⅛-in.
high; wt., 7 oz., 1 tomato 40
Canned, solids and liquid, 1 cup ... 50
Tomato catsup:
Cup, 1 cup 290
Tablespoon, 1 tablespoon 15
Tomato juice, canned:
Cup, 1 cup 45
Glass (6 fl. oz.), 1 glass 35

Turnips, cooked diced, 1 cup 35
Turnip greens, cooked, 1 cup 30

FRUITS AND FRUIT PRODUCTS

Apples, raw (about 3 per
pound), 1 apple 70
Apple juice, bottled or
canned, 1 cup 120
Applesauce, canned:
Unsweetened, 1 cup 100
Apricots:
Raw (about 12 per lb.),
3 apricots 55
Dried, uncooked (40 halves per
cup), 1 cup 390
Cooked, unsweetened, fruit and
liquid, 1 cup 240
Apricot nectar, canned, 1 cup..... 140

Avocados, whole fruit, raw:
California (mid- and late-winter;
diam. 3⅛-in.), 1 avocado........ 370
Florida (late summer, fall;
diam. 3⅜-in.), 1 avocado........ 390

Bananas, raw, medium size,
1 banana 100
Banana flakes, 1 cup............. 340
Blackberries, raw, 1 cup.......... 85
Blueberries, raw, 1 cup........... 85
Cantaloups, raw; medium, 5-in. diam.
about 1⅔ lbs., ½ melon 60

Cherries, canned, red, sour, pitted,
water pack, 1 cup 105

Cranberry juice cocktail,
canned, 1 cup................... 165

Figs, dried, large, 2x1-in., 1 fig ... 60

Fruit cocktail, canned, in
water, ½ cup.................... 50

Grapefruit:
Raw, medium, 3¾-in. diam.:
White, ½ grapefruit............ 45
Pink or red, ½ grapefruit 50
Grapefruit juice:
Fresh, 1 cup 95
Canned, white:
Unsweetened, 1 cup 100
Frozen, concentrate, unsweetened:
Undiluted, can 6 fl. oz., 1 can..... 300
Diluted with 3 parts water by
volume, 1 cup................. 100

Grapes, raw:
American type (slip skin), 1 cup ... 65
European type (adherent
skin), 1 cup.................... 95

Grape juice:
Canned or bottled, 1 cup 165
Frozen concentrate, sweetened:
Undiluted, can, 6 fl. oz., 1 can 395
Diluted with 3 parts water by
volume, 1 cup................. 135
Grape juice drink, 1 cup.......... 135

Lemons, raw, 2⅛-in. diam., size
165. Used for juice, 1 lemon...... 20
Lemon juice, raw, 1 cup.......... 60
Lemonade concentrate:
  Frozen, 6 fl. oz. per can, 1 can 430
  Diluted with 4⅓ parts water,
  by volume, 1 cup............... 110
Lime juice:
  Fresh, 1 cup 65
  Canned, unsweetened, 1 cup..... 65
Limeade concentrate, frozen:
  Undiluted, can, 6 fl. oz., 1 can ... 410
  Diluted with 4⅓ parts water,
  by volume, 1 cup............... 100

Oranges, raw, 2⅝-in. diam., all
commercial, varieties, 1 orange ... 65
Orange juice, fresh, all varieties,
1 cup 110
  Canned, unsweetened, 1 cup..... 120
  Frozen concentrate:
  Undiluted, can, 6 fl. oz., 1 can 330
  Diluted with 3 parts water by
  volume, 1 cup................. 110

Dehydrated crystals, 4 oz......... 430
  Prepared with water (1 lb. yields
  about 1 gallon), 1 cup........... 115
Orange-apricot juice drink, 1 cup ... 125
Orange and grapefruit juice:
  Frozen concentrate:
  Undiluted, can, 6 fl. oz., 1 can 330
  Diluted with 3 parts water by
  volume, 1 cup................. 110

Papayas, raw, ½-in. cubes, 1 cup.... 70

Peaches:
  Raw:
  Whole, medium, 2-in. diam.,
  about 4 per lb., 1 peach 35
  Sliced, 1 cup.................. 65
  Canned, yellow-fleshed, solids
  and liquid:
  Water pack, 1 cup............. 75
  Dried, uncooked, 1 cup 420
  Cooked, unsweetened, 10-12 halves
  and juice, 1 cup 220
  Frozen:
  Carton, 12 oz. not thawed,
  1 carton 300

Pears:
  Raw, 3x2½-in. diam., 1 pear..... 100
  Canned, solids and liquid:
  Packed in water: Halves or
  slices, ½ cup................. 50

Pineapple:
  Raw, diced, 1 cup 75
Pineapple juice, canned, 1 cup 135

Plums, all except prunes:
  Raw, 2-in. diam., about 2 oz.
  1 plum 25
Prunes, dried, "softenized",
medium:

Uncooked, 4 prunes 70
Cooked, unsweetened, 17-18 prunes
and ⅓ cup liquid, 1 cup 295
Prune juice, canned or bottled,
1 cup 200

Raisins, seedless:
  Packaged, ½ oz. or 1½ tablespoon
  per package, 1 package.......... 40
  Cup, pressed down, 1 cup 480

Raspberries, red:
  Raw, 1 cup 70
  Frozen, 10-oz. carton, not
  thawed, 1 carton 275

Strawberries:
  Raw, capped, 1 cup............. 55
  Frozen, 10-oz. carton, not
  thawed, 1 carton 310

Tangerines, raw, medium, 2⅜-in.
diam., size 176, 1 tangerine....... 40

Watermelon, raw, wedge, 4x8-in.
1/16 of 10x16-in. melon, about
2 lbs. with rind, 1 wedge 115

GRAIN PRODUCTS

Bagel, 3-in. diam:
  Egg, 1 bagel 165
  Water, 1 bagel 165
Barley, pearled, light
uncooked, 1 cup................. 700

Bran flakes (40% bran), added
thiamin and iron, 1 cup 105

Bran flakes with raisins, added
thiamin and iron, 1 cup 145

Breads:
  Boston brown bread, slice
  3x¾ in., 1 slice................ 100
  Cracked-wheat bread:
  Loaf, 1 lb., 1 loaf............ 1,190
  Slice, 18 slices per loaf, 1 slice... 65
  Raisin bread:
  Loaf, 1 lb., 1 loaf............ 1,190
  Slice, 18 slices per loaf, 1 slice... 65
  Rye bread:
  American, light (⅓ rye, ⅔ wheat):
  Loaf, 1 lb., 1 loaf........... 1,100
  Slice, 18 slices per loaf, 1 slice.... 60
  Pumpernickel:
  Loaf, 1 lb., 1 loaf........... 1,115
  White bread, enriched:
  Soft-crumb type:
  Loaf, 1 lb., 1 loaf.......... 1,225
  Slice, 18 slices per loaf, 1 slice.... 70
  Slice, 22 slices per loaf, 1 slice.... 55
  Slice, toasted, 1 slice 55
  Loaf, 1½ lbs., 1 loaf 1,835
  Slice, 24 slices per loaf, 1 slice.... 75
  Slice, toasted, 1 slice 75
  Slice, 28 slices per loaf........ 65
  Slice toasted, 1 slice 65

Firm-crumb type:
Loaf, 1 lb., 1 loaf............ 1,245
Slice, 20 slices per loaf, 1 slice... 65
Slice, toasted, 1 slice 65
Loaf, 2 lbs., 1 loaf............ 2,495
Slice, 34 slices per loaf, 1 slice... 75
Slice, toasted, 1 slice 75

Whole wheat bread, soft-crumb type:
Loaf, 1 lb., 1 loaf............. 1,095
Slice, 16 slices per loaf, 1 slice.... 65
Slice, toasted, 1 slice 65

Whole wheat bread, firm-crumb type:
Loaf, 1 lb., 1 loaf............ 1,100
Slice, 18 slice per loaf, 1 slice ... 60
Slice, toasted, 1 slice 60

Breadcrumbs, dry, grated, 1 cup... 390

Buckwheat flour, light,
sifted, 1 cup 340

Bulgur, canned, seasoned, 1 cup... 245

Corn (hominy) grits, degermed,
cooked:
Enriched, 1 cup 125
Unenriched, 1 cup.............. 125

Corn meal:
Whole-ground, unbolted, dry
1 cup 435
Bolted (nearly whole-grain),
dry, 1 cup 440
Degermed, enriched:
Dry form, 1 cup............... 500
Cooked, 1 cup 120
Degermed, unenriched:
Dry form, 1 cup............... 500
Cooked, 1 cup 120

Corn muffins, made with enriched
degermed corn meal and enriched
flour, muffin 2⅜-in. diam.,
1 muffin....................... 125

Corn muffins, made with mix, egg
and milk, muffin 2⅜-in. diam.,
1 muffin....................... 130

Crackers:
Kavli, 1 cracker 70
Finn-Crisp, 1 cracker 20

Farina, quick-cooking, enriched,
cooked, 1 cup.................. 105

Macaroni, whole wheat.............

Oats (with or without corn) puffed,
added nutrients, 1 cup 100

Oatmeal or rolled oats, cooked
1 cup 130

Pancakes, 4-in. diam.:
Wheat, enriched flour (home
recipe), 1 cake 60
Buckwheat (make from mix with egg
and milk), 1 cake 55
Plain or buttermilk (made from
mix with egg and milk), 1 cake.... 60

Popcorn, popped:
Plain, large kernel, 1 cup 25
With oil and salt, 1 cup 40
Sugar coated, 1 cup............. 135

Pretzels:
Dutch, twisted, 1 pretzel 60
Thin, twisted, 1 pretzel........... 25
Stick, small, 2¼ in., 10 sticks 10
Stick, regular, 3⅛ in., 5 sticks..... 10

Rice, white:
Enriched:
Raw, 1 cup.................... 670
Cooked, 1 cup 225
Instant, ready-to-serve, 1 cup ... 180
Unenriched, cooked, 1 cup 225
Parboiled, cooked, 1 cup 185

Rice, puffed, added nutrients,
1 cup 60

Rye wafers, whole-grain,
1⅞x 3½ in., 2 wafers............. 45

Spaghetti, whole wheat, 2 oz...... 202

Wheat, puffed, added nutrients,
1 cup 55

Wheat, shredded, plain, 1 biscuit ... 90
Wheat flakes, added nutrients,
1 cup 105

Wheat flours:
Whole wheat, from hard wheats,
stirred, 1 cup 400
All-purpose or family flour,
enriched:
Sifted, 1 cup.................. 420
Unsifted, 1 cup 455
Self-rising, enriched, 1 cup 440
Cake or pastry flour, sifted
1 cup 350

FATS, OILS

Margarine:
Regular, 4 sticks per pound:
Stick, ½ cup 815
Tablespoon (approx. ⅛ stick),
1 tablespoon.................. 100
Pat (1-in. sq. ⅓-in. high; 90
per pound), 1 pat............... 35
Whipped, 6 sticks per pound:
Stick, ½ cup 545

Oils, salad or cooking:
Corn, 1 cup.................. 1,945
1 tablespoon.............. 125
Cottonseed, 1 cup 1,945
1 tablespoon 125
Olive, 1 cup................. 1,945
1 tablespoon.............. 125
Peanut, 1 cup................ 1,945
1 tablespoon 125
Safflower, 1 cup............. 1,945
1 tablespoon 125
Soybean, 1 cup............... 1,945
1 tablespoon............ 125

SUGARS, SWEETS

Honey, strained or extracted,
1 tablespoon 65

Sugars:
Brown, firm packed, 1 cup 820

MISCELLANEOUS ITEMS

Beverages, alcoholic:
Beer, 12 fl. oz. 150
Gin, rum, vodka, whiskey:
80-proof, 1½ fl. oz., jigger 100
86-proof, 1½ fl. oz., jigger 105
90-proof, 1½ fl. oz., jigger 110
94-proof, 1½ fl. oz., jigger 115
100-proof, 1½ fl. oz., jigger 125
Wines:
Dessert, 3½ fl. oz. glass 140
Table, 3½ fl. oz. glass 85

Beverages, carbonated, sweetened, nonalcoholic:
Carbonated water, 12 fl. oz. 115
Cola type, 12 fl. oz. 145
Fruit-flavored sodas and Tom
Collins mixes, 12 fl. oz. 170
Ginger ale, 12 fl. oz. 115
Root beer, 12 fl. oz. 150

Bouillon cubes, approx. ½ in.,
1 cube 5

Chocolate:
Bitter or baking, 1 oz. 145

Gelatin:
Plain, dry powder in envelope,
1 envelope 25
Dessert powder, 3-oz. pkg.,
1 pkg. 315
Gelatin dessert, prepared with
water, 1 cup 140

Olives, pickled:
Green, 4 medium 15
(or 3 extra large or 2 giant)
Ripe: Mission, 3 small 15
(or 2 large)

Pickles, cucumber:
Dill, medium, whole, 3¾-in. long,
1¼ in. diam., 1 pickle 10
Fresh, sliced, 1½ in. diam.,
¼ in. thick, 2 slices 10
Sweet, gherkin, small, whole, approx.
2½ in. long, ¾ in. diam.,
1 pickle 20
Relish, finely chopped, sweet
1 tablespoon 20

Popsicle, 3 fl. oz. size, 1 popsicle ... 70
Vinegar, 1 tablespoon 2

Yeast:
Baker's, dry, active, 1 package 20
Brewer's, dry, 1 tablespoon 25

IDEAL WEIGHT CHART

HEIGHT	WOMEN (weight in pounds)	MEN (weight in pounds)
4'10"	90-98	95-105
4'11"	93-102	98-108
5'	95-105	100-111
5'1"	97-108	105-117
5'2"	100-111	110-123
5'3"	105-118	115-128
5'4"	110-123	120-133
5'5"	112-126	125-138
5'6"	117-130	130-143
5'7"	120-134	133-148
5'8"	125-139	137-153
5'9"	130-144	143-159
5'10"	135-149	148-164
5'11"	140-154	152-168
6'	144-158	155-171
6'1"		163-179
6'2"		167-183
6'3"		170-195
6'4"		178-198
6'5"		

INDEX

207